FORTY JOBS IN FORTY YEARS

And a few cashies on the side...

STEPHEN PHILLIPS

TheBookStudio

All correspondence to the author:
Phone: 0419 668 345

© Copyright Stephen Phillips

First Printed 2021

The right of Stephen Phillips to be identified as the author of this work has been asserted by him in accordance with the Copyright, Designs and Patents act.

All rights reserved. No part of this publication may be reproduced, stored in or introduced into a retrieval system, or transmitted, in any form, or by any means (electronic, mechanical, photocopying, recording or otherwise) without the prior written permission of the publisher. Any person who does any unauthorised act in relation to this publication may be liable to criminal prosecution and civil claims for damages.

This book is sold subject to the condition that it shall not, by way of trade or otherwise, be lent, re-sold, hired out, or otherwise circulated without the publisher's prior consent in any form of binding or cover other than that in which it is published and without a similar condition including this condition being imposed on the subsequent purchaser.

ISBN: 978-0-6487858-4-2

Proudly produced by

www.thebookstudio.com.au

*Dedicated to my grandfather,
Albert James Septimus Phillips,
who worked in dangerous situations
to earn his money.*

Introduction

I suppose a pre-emptory word is necessary when recalling parts of my life which may impact on other people and although I don't remember all the names of the people I worked with, or for, I mean to cause no slight on anyone by recalling these stories.

If you are fortunate enough to be reading this and realise that you are one of them please take it in the vein it was intended, with some humour and, on reflection, a period in our lives where we were (and still are) trying to find our place in the world.

I have avoided writing all these jobs in chronological order and intend on jumping huge time spans forwards and backwards. Every job mentioned is something that I was paid for from pocket money to a six figure salary and although some jobs lasted over thirty years, others may have been a one off, one day wonder.

There were dozens of jobs involving music which clocks me well over the forty mark but I have decided to just list the more memorable ones. Some jobs I was sacked from and some I quit but there was only ever a two week period in my whole life where I obtained government support to live, however, I'll elaborate on that at some point. So, in no particular order…

'Adaptation is the key to survival.'

The Brisbane Club was a fine institution catering for the rich and uber-rich. Lawyers, doctors, bankers, stockbrokers, old and new money made up the membership of this exclusive club. The waiting list to become a member was over six years from when you were nominated and vouched for by other members, to being invited into the club. No doubt, some were lucky enough to leap-frog this process, depending on their kind donations to the furtherance of this elite congregation. I was about to become a member...of the staff.

I had just been 'let go' from a position in a finance company and had been studying hospitality in the evenings. Tom, who ran the course, was an older gentleman with years of experience in the hospitality industry. I had an enormous amount of respect for him as he valued old fashioned service, dignity and pride and made me always remember never to lower my standards no matter where I worked. After a few weeks, it appeared I had a natural flair for the silver service side of hospitality and became a deft hand at wine service and bar work and received my graduation certificate.

I saw the job advertised in the Courier Mail asking for an experienced steward and turned up at the Brisbane Club appropriately dressed.

At the end of a long table in a dark, regent-green room sat Hugh, the Maître D of the club. He looked at my resume briefly and was about to dismiss me because I had little experience. I assured him that I was competent and willing to work and offered my services for a trial period. I said, "If I don't live up to your standards sir, I'll gladly seek employment elsewhere" or some other bullshit like that. I smiled at him and for a brief moment he hesitated then said, "Ok, be here at eleven to do the lunch til three and we'll see how you go." He stood quickly, shook my hand and I thanked him profusely for allowing me a chance.

At 10:45 I was up the lift and walking through the magnificent old world architecture of the club with its beautifully decorated high ceilings, chandeliers and Doric pillars. Large leadlight windows faced onto what is now Post Office Square. I was introduced to a tall, darkhaired German steward called Richard who was austere and held himself with a ramrod straight back. He looked me up and down and said, "Follow me." We walked upstairs to the steward's room and selected an appropriately fitted vest with the club logo over the left breast, adjusted my black bow tie and ensured I had my wine knife and order book. He explained that I would be tending the stock exchange table and they were very particular about how they were served. "Take the drink orders to the bar, make sure all the tables have the correct glasses and cutlery in the correct place and don't ever stand around doing nothing unless you are told to." Richard was curt but I respected his professionalism and experience. The first members began to drift in around eleven thirty and I looked to Richard for guidance. He would occasionally whisper something to me and I would be on high alert as to every situation that required attention. The members expected perfection.

As I served my first drinks in the club one of the members asked me who I was and I said I had just started today. He didn't like it. He asked Hugh if he could have Richard serving the table and so both Richard and I worked as a team on this table of grumpy old rich men. I did get to serve others in the room when required and noticed a few prominent politicians and high flyers in the legal world knobbing in with a table full of clients. One particularly flamboyant lawyer, who used to wear a different brightly coloured bow tie every day, always ordered Mumms champagne to impress his clients. Quite often there was at least a bottle or two left over for the stewards. I served food, cleared plates, poured water, procured drinks from the bar, opened and poured wine and was beginning to enjoy the whole experience. One of the older stock exchange fellows had consumed his usual ration of whiskey, red and white wine and a few sneaky ones in between when he called me over to ask for some Grandfathers Port. His four friends at the table thought that was a grand idea and they also ordered one. As I walked back from the bar with over two hundred dollars' worth of fortified wine on my tray I leaned over to place one in front of the gentleman to my right and tipped two of the glasses which fell onto the tray and spilled onto the trousers of the cranky man who had not wanted me serving him. He looked up in disgust and I apologised profusely. His face went red with indignation and he glanced at his fellow diners.

I assured them I would replace the port and attend to his stain and placed a napkin over his leg. He growled something at me and then looked for Hugh as if to say, 'He's no good.'

Richard stepped in quickly with a small can of soda water, poured it onto the stain and began to pat it out with a napkin while the gentleman continued his conversation. I was sweating and thought that would be the end of me at the Brisbane Club. As we drew towards the three o'clock clean up, Richard and Hugh approached me.

"Stephen that was an unfortunate accident at the Stock Exchange table today but the rest of the time you worked well. Come and see me after the clean-up and we'll see what's coming up this week. Richard said you were a promising steward and we are short of people at the moment." Hugh turned and left me with Richard and I thanked him for vouching for me.

In the stewards room Richard poured us the remnants of a bottle of Dom Perignon which one of the members had not finished and toasted my first day. "That was good really," he said with not much emotion on his face (but I could tell he was happy to have me there.) "Some of our stewards were chefs and they didn't want to cook any more but they can't serve either and they always look messy." He raised his glass to me and I tasted Dom Perignon for the first time. We also helped ourselves to the rest of that day's buffet which was extravagant to say the least. That lunch meal became standard operating procedure and I ate like a prince as there were always baked hams, roast turkeys and exotic seafood.

As I was leaving, Hugh took me aside and explained that I would be working that night and on the weekend. I was ecstatic. He gave me a roster showing who I would be working with and what the occasion may be for each of them. Sometimes a private birthday party for a member's wife or children; others were retirement dinners or celebrations of some kind.

I quickly had to adjust my social calendar to suit as I knew I could excel in this job. It was exciting and I felt a surge of confidence as I walked home past the Eternal Flame memorial dragging on a Marlboro red.

As the weeks and months skipped along I gained the confidence of Hugh to the point where he would ask me to serve at private functions in the club and at members' houses. He would say, "Stephen, Mr Such and Such has asked that you serve his party at Yerongapilly. He likes your service at the club and you will be paid cash for anything outside the club plus your normal wage from us." My eyes popped when I realised how much money I could make for a few hours work. It was challenging at times but I enjoyed the human interaction and seeing the other side of life where real wealth was thrown around like cheap opinions.

Richard had been at the club for a long time and he told me he was going back to Germany for a while to visit family and possibly work. He told me I would probably get all the private functions that he used to have exclusively under his belt (or cummerbund).

I therefore, wasn't shocked when Hugh had elevated me to a preferred position serving politicians, doctors and lawyers at their homes. One of these soirees was at a well-known doctor's residence in Indooroopilly. I arrived at five dressed for action with bow tie and club vest and began to prepare trays of champagne, wine and beer for the arriving guests. The club had already delivered the eskies and trays for the event and would pick them up the next day. All I had to do was make sure everyone had a drink in their hand and I roamed the rooms with a silver tray balanced on my right hand refilling glasses and making sure late arrivals also had welcome drinks. When the food service was to start with trays of canapes and finger food, a young waitress from the club would arrive and help me serve. She was there for only an hour or so and then left.

One of the late arrivals was the very affable Brisbane Mayor, Sally-Anne Atkinson. At the door she took off her uncomfortable heels and strode up the front stairs. I asked if she would like champagne and she said, "Ooh, I'd love a beer." She drank half the glass in one go and then proceeded to talk to me for a few minutes wanting to know my name and where I came from and my family. Aware that I was abandoning my duties, I excused myself and as I left she waived her empty glass at me for a refill.

By nine o'clock or so most of the guests had left and the doctor hosting the party pulled me aside to write a cheque for my services. He'd had a few by this time and he congratulated me on my work. The fee was supposed to be a hundred dollars but he wrote the cheque for two hundred and fifty. I thanked him and drove home. The next time I saw the waitress at the club I gave her fifty dollars cash and I explained to her that it was a bonus for the doctor's party. She looked at me in shock and said, "Did you keep some for yourself?"

On another occasion at the club I served in a small room where six men were seated about a round polished mahogany table. The man in charge was large, very rotund with a red face and a hundred and fifty kilos of stomach. I was serving the lunch they had chosen and noticed plans on the table for a bridge project. It was the Main Roads Minister with the planning committee for the building of the Gateway Bridge. I felt privileged to have been witness to this plan and had begun to tell people about it two years before it got off the ground. Of course no one believed me at the time. The minister had left me a tip on his bread and butter plate. I showed Hugh and he said, "That's for you." It was very uncharacteristic for this man but I slipped the generous bonus into my vest pocket.

Another politician, from the Joh era, whose name I shall not reveal, had a private function for his birthday and had twenty or so guests in the back room. They had been drinking in the bar on arrival but I was led to believe that he had been drinking since lunchtime. While I roamed the table I kept an eye on him as his wife was whispering into his ear about something. He looked pretty pissed and I immediately brought water for everyone at the table beginning with the politician and his wife.

She said, "Thankyou Stephen, that's a wonderful idea." She moved several wine bottles out of his reach and I followed her lead by removing them to the cabinet at the back of the room. He became incensed and bellowed for a drink which led his wife to admonish him. He looked at her with his bloodshot eyes and went to stand to go to the bar. As he rose he tripped on the chair and was inevitably going to hit the ground in an embarrassing display of 'flagrant wastage of public funds' when I stepped forward and intercepted him, easing him back into his chair. He became belligerent. I asked his wife if she would like me to call a taxi and she again thanked me using my first name. The meal was pretty much over and the other guests thought it would be polite to forego dessert and port. They moved towards the inside bar as I managed to get the politician and his wife safely to the lift. As the lift door opened she handed something to me which I kept in the palm of my hand. "Thank you again Stephen," she said with a rather embarrassed smile. As I returned to clean up the table I looked down at the hundred dollar bill. The next day I gave the waitress another thirty dollars to which she replied, "Did you keep any for yourself?"

On many occasions there were twenty-first birthdays celebrated in the club. The members would hire out a huge space for the evening and all the family and friends would stand around gabbling like over-dressed flamingos at a cocktail party. I had a tray of Grasshoppers and Brandy Alexanders which I was trying to distribute evenly amongst the crowd when one of the friends of the birthday girl cornered me and began sculling drinks straight off the tray and returning the empties. I tried to slow him down but he was a typical spoilt brat private school boy who grabbed two drinks off the tray at a time when, the mother of the birthday girl said, "Oh, Jeremy. There's no need for that. There's plenty more." He slunk away trying to say to her that he was getting one for his girlfriend. I looked at him realising that we knew each other and said, "Sprung Jeremy," and smiled as I moved off to the rest of the crowd. He grabbed me roughly by one elbow nearly knocking the remaining two drinks off the tray and sneered at me, "Shut up, you're just hired help." Needless to say he further embarrassed himself by blurting something out during the speeches. One of his sober friends had got him just inside the toilet door before he projectile vomited on the man exiting the toilets only to find that it was the birthday girl's father. Calmly, the father gave Jeremy's friend some money to put his miscreant friend in a taxi, procured a fresh shirt and jacket from Hugh (which he always kept in reserve) and rejoined the party. At the end of the festivities I was invited to serve at their Christmas party in a few weeks and noticed that Jeremy was nowhere to be seen. Again, a healthy cash bonus accompanied both events.

On a few occasions, some of the stewards were approached by very rich and very drunk women who asked for a 'slow and comfortable screw against the wall' (a drink, by the way, for those of you who may not realize). For some, that was a perk of the job. For others, they just made the Southern Comfort based drink and left. The rich get stupidly drunk too.

An elderly member of the club had invited his family to celebrate his wife's seventieth birthday. He was a well-respected business man who was always polite and treated the staff with true respect. When the family had gathered in the front bar for pre-dinner drinks I escorted them to their seats and proceeded to take orders. I went to the bar and began to make the drinks when the day manager, a beautiful young blonde German woman, came over to assist me. "Where is the list?" she asked. I pointed to my head and began to rattle off the simpler drinks for her, which included three beers, two pink lemonades and a brandy on ice. The rest I mixed or poured myself and then returned with my tray to deliver the drinks to the correct people. After I had served the member last he turned to me and said, "I saw what you did then. You took thirteen orders without writing them down and delivered all the drinks to the right people. Extraordinary, I'm going to mention it to Hugh."

"Thankyou sir, I appreciate your kind comments." I served their dinner in a small side room. The décor and food reminded me of a palace in seventeenth century France where the royal family would dine. The gentleman did mention it to Hugh and at some point I received a pay rise and many more requests from people to serve at their private functions. The kind member also left me a very healthy tip at the end of the night which I didn't have to share with anyone. When I got home late at night, I drank and wrote observational poems.

There were many memorable dinners I served like that and I learned how to flambé 'crepe suzette' at the tables and rescue reticent corks from ancient wine bottles. I visited the cellar several times and it was one of those typical underground dirt floor types with pipes and water dripping through the whole length of the underground part of the building. I got to know the cellarman well enough to purchase a bottle of 1966 Dow port from Portugal as an investment but that's another story connected with another job. Alan and Dave? Tontine?

The people I met in those eighteen months or so were 'mostly' wonderful people. There were a dozen or so frantic and cantankerous chefs, stewards who came and went because they didn't like the weekend work or couldn't keep up with the high standards that Hugh set. One of the stewards, Nick Jovic (not sure it's his real name) worked with me on some huge nights at the club like The Annual Air Navigators Guild dinner with special guest speaker, Australian author, Morris West. I had the job at the top two tables of eight including Morris West and at some time in the proceedings I asked for an autograph on the dinner menu. I told him I was an aspiring writer and he engaged me briefly before he signed the menu with my waiters pencil; 'With all good wishes' Morris West.' I still have it today tucked away in my drawer of memories. He rose to give his specially crafted address to the Air Navigators Guild and all the stewards posted themselves quietly near a wall. I was nearest to him and listened carefully as he spoke. To my amazement, he was hilarious, but no one in the room realised what he had said until I began to laugh and applaud at the same time.

He looked at me and smiled and I couldn't help but feel his pain at not being able to crack this tough crowd. The Air Navigators then trickled in with applause and a few mumbled 'what'd he say'. He was a consummate orator and I had a renewed respect for him and less for the seemingly ignorant membership of the Air Navigators Guild. It was a long night for Morris. After clean up, Nick and I polished off the remnants of some vintage '73 Penfolds Grange (he didn't know what it was) and decided to go out for a drink, sans bowties.

We walked around the corner to Rosie's bar, went upstairs and ordered a jug of beer and then realised neither of us had any money. The girl behind the bar spotted our black and whites and shouted us a jug. "I'll be with you in a minute boys, I'm just finishing up." She did indeed finish, because it was around eleven thirty and bought another jug with her to sit with us. I think she fancied Nick because he was a reasonably good looking guy and we drank several jugs with her and her friends before we left to go home. "Come with us. We're going to another bar round the corner," the girl from Rosie's said. We did and drank again for free after telling our story of the Air Navigators Guild dinner. Well, I told the story and Nick was listening quietly while the girl from Rosie's hung on to his biceps. Admittedly, he did look a bit like a Russian version of Sean Bean. They kissed and exchanged numbers.

By one o'clock we wandered towards my house at Spring Hill but were distracted by a restaurant that I used to haunt called 'The Agency' in Upper Edward Street. I walked in expecting to see some staff I knew but it was not the case. We tried to tell the young girl at the bar that we had just finished work, mentioned one of the other staff members who were absent, and we'd pay her tomorrow but she wouldn't have a bar of it.

Just as we were about to walk out a man came to the bar and recognised us. "Hey, you guysh were jusht sherving at the dinner at the Brishbane Club." We nodded and he said to the girl behind the bar, "Give them anyshing they want on my tab." He smiled and shook our hands and we ordered Galliano shots for the next half an hour while getting to know the girl behind the bar. Before we left she handed me a bottle of Galliano to take with us and put it on the kind man's tab saying, "He won't know." Nick and I walked back to my house and cracked the bottle, drinking until the sun came up and laughing at how we had been able to drink all night without any money. At dawn I tapped the menu in my pocket signed by Morris West and was inspired to write then and there before the effects of the Galliano ran out. Nick walked out the door and somehow made his way home. I never saw him again.

Eventually, the Brisbane Club was relocated to the Qantas building in Adelaide Street while renovations were underway at the club. Most staff were temporarily laid off until the reno was completed. In the meantime I had to find work, and so, with a small tear in my eye and some fond memories, I left behind the Brisbane Club with its' beautiful architecture and old world charm. It still operates as a high-end club with fine dining, private functions and cellar tours. Hugh did eventually ask me back but I'd found another job and sadly had to refuse.

'Sometimes in life...
you just have to get your hands dirty.'

One of the more physical jobs I had was building rock retaining walls out at Silverton Creek just below Somerset Dam. I had met this beautiful Italian girl at my previous job and her father offered for me to go with him to build these walls for the main roads department. He had obviously underquoted the job because we started with four of us originally, three Italians and myself, and after the first two days the other Italians quit saying it wasn't worth the money.

Franco and I were left with the task of breaking up rocks and fitting them neatly into a twenty two metre long wall on both sides of the creek. The base was three metres wide tapering to about one metre at the top. The total height was about three metres. He had quoted them what he thought was per cubic metre and said it would take us about three months. Well, you cannot imagine a more daunting task in the middle of a stinking humid creek with very little breeze to cool us down.

We had an old fashioned petrol driven cement mixer, two shovels, two trowels, two pairs of gloves, a fifteen pound sledgehammer, a wheel barrow and a homemade tin chute to pour the concrete into the wall. I broke rocks into smaller, easier-to-handle pieces, mixed the concrete in batches, tipped it into the wheelbarrow and carted it to where Franco would place the rocks carefully into the wall using a somewhat higgledy-piggledy string line. He was very particular about how the rock face would look, fitting each piece carefully to keep the slope on a gradual rise and yet somehow make it a work of art. Behind the wall we would load rocks to fill the void behind the face and it would grow slowly each day into an effective water-resistant masterpiece. The main roads guys wanted us to hurry up but Franco was too proud of his work.

I was reasonably fit when I started this job as I had been practicing martial arts and Tai Chi, so I relished the physical work and realised the shovelling and rock breaking would keep me quite healthy despite our hourly smoke breaks sucking down a B&H with a sip of water.

We lodged at the Toogoolawa Pub for the duration which was about thirty kilometres from the job site. This was supposed to save us the drive back to Brisbane every day but I think Franco was happy to be away from his wife for a while as he said in his Italo-English, "Steef, my wife, he makea my balls swell up", and he would laugh until his smoke-rattled lungs merged into a guttural cough of phlegm which he would then spit into the wall.

Nobody worked harder than Franco. We would rise at 4:30, before breakfast was served in the pub, help ourselves to raw eggs from the kitchen (I diluted mine in a glass of milk) and drive his red F100 ute to the site before anyone else appeared. Franco would have his mandatory smokes on rising and two on the trip there. He would then issue vague orders which I had already begun. The air was crisp and the creek was quiet until I began the mixer.

We did eventually remember to bring a flask of water with us when we realised how hot it was and how far we were from running water that was potable despite the fact that Somerset Dam was just 200 metres from where we were working. I broke rocks and mixed concrete and barrowed it to where Franco was carefully placing the face of the wall. The main roads department would dump rocks down the hill for us to use and occasionally and rather carelessly we would have to duck out of the way as stray rocks sped over the wall. Franco was ropeable and let them have a mouthful in Italian and I would translate to the laughing workers above us who ensured it wouldn't happen again. A lot of the time, one of the lazy road workers would stand above the wall and watch us working whilst making snide and sometimes racist comments about Franco and myself. There was nothing harmful in it and I didn't react because I knew how much of an idiot he was. I ignored him completely.

At morning tea I would go up to the local shop and get coffee flavoured milk and sausage rolls or pies. Lunch was again a cigarette and water and we worked until 5 each day. A twelve hour day, every day for three months, but we were not going to finish in the time allotted us. Back at the pub on dark we would drink three pots of beer before a massive pub dinner was served at the bar. Franco would usually go straight to bed but I felt like I could have stayed up for a few more hours and often ended up in the back bar watching the locals play pool. There were three girls who seemed to be at the pub most nights and one of them approached me for a game which I accepted. She was a plump girl with a round face full of freckles and a mane of bright ginger hair. She asked me what I was doing here and as I explained, the other two girls leaned in to listen. One was a thin, part aboriginal girl with tattoos and a few teeth missing. The other was dark haired and surly, rarely smiling and said very little. I had to leave most nights before 9 so I could get enough sleep for the next day's hard yakka. My hands were beginning to blister and stung when the soap hit them in the cold shower. Sometimes I would find a pencil and piece of paper and write something vaguely poetic to help me sleep. Where they ended up, who could tell? In the glovebox?

The next day Franco realised we were getting behind and needed some extra labour. We ventured back to Brisbane for the Christmas break and I asked my brother-in-law Laurie, who was studying law at the time, if he wanted to earn a few extra dollars. He said he would be delighted and I explained what he would be doing. He seemed to accept the challenge but when we actually got back to the site, he realised he had committed himself to the equivalent of a forced labour camp and I could see the dread filling his face when he realised what was involved. He had never really done any labouring work and I initially put him on the cement mixer while I helped Franco with the face of the wall. In between mixing and laying the rocks we would break up bigger rocks with the sledge hammer. After a while Laurie started to see the lighter side of what we were doing and he told the main roads workers that I was an Australian Martial Arts champion.

They always looked at me differently from then on but I told them Laurie was a middle weight boxing champion and they rarely dumped stray rocks down the slope after that, making sure they were carefully placed where we could reach them. The work was hot, humid and physical for twelve, and sometimes more, hours a day. We were getting unintentionally tanned and toned and to compensate for the physical work and isolation from our homes, we developed a sense of humour about what we were doing, sometimes taking the piss out of the road crew who took it as good as they gave. There were cows everywhere in the paddocks around us and Laurie would wave his shovel at them mooing.

We made slow progress for the next two weeks but it looked like the end might be near. Laurie had to leave to go back to Law School and Franco paid him what I thought was way too much for his two weeks of service but he had come to like Laurie and his quirky little jokes about Franco ('Santa Maria' he would say). He threatened the main roads crew with his shovel a couple of times gesturing to stick the handle up their arse. It was in good humour though and they all laughed. Once again, it was back to Franco and me.

We worked through the hottest part of January and into February always being hurried up by the main roads gang. On one occasion I thought I had sliced my finger off after lifting the aluminium chute towards the wall. Franco had adjusted it from his end not realising my fingers were still underneath it and I bellowed for him to move it quickly. He raced up the wall to see the damage but to my amazement, and his, I only had a serious bruise at the base of my finger. I think the callouses I had worked up on both my hands had saved the metal from puncturing my skin, although I did wear gloves most of the time after the first painful week of raw blisters.

We sort of rushed the last few metres of the wall which was not as visible from the road or the creek and after a final few 12 hour days we stood back to look at our handy-work. There was blood, sweat and urine in that wall; and spit and rubbish we should have put into a bin. We loaded all the tools and mixer into the truck and went to the 'donger' to calculate the payment. As I mentioned before, Franco had rather underestimated the volume of the wall but had quoted $55 per cubic metre. In his mind, he had only used a linear metre in his guestimations but I was quick to take a calculator from one of the main roads engineers and punch in the numbers correctly. Franco's quote was going to be only about three thousand dollars but I quickly stepped in to translate between him and the MRD guys and worked it into six and a half thousand dollars. They agreed and we climbed into the truck to head home with a cheque which was hardly going to pay for the cost of our hard labours. I eventually received about $2500 because Franco had paid for the pub accommodation, meals and beers and he had already paid Laurie a handsome sum. At the end of it Franco would not have much left but he was proud of his work and I think I had showed him that I was capable of doing an honest day's work that wasn't in an office. The wall still stands at Silverton Creek below the road heading towards Somerset Dam from Esk.

> 'There are only four types
> of people in the world:
> imbeciles, cretins, morons and fools.
> When you work out who the other three are,
> you will know which one is you.'

Twice in my long list of jobs I delivered advertising leaflets to letter boxes. The first time came about because my brother and I wanted to earn some pocket money. A family friend, Tony, had organised the leaflets in the boot of his car and drove to Arana Hills where he would drop us at one end of a very long road. Taking a side each we would walk then run along with a fully stuffed airline bag over our shoulders carefully trying to shove them into letter boxes. Despite refusals from owners and the impending dog danger (in those days dogs were not tethered or fenced in and we would often have to run to the other side of the road to avoid being bitten) we would meet Tony at the end of the road and he would then drop us at another long road (Patricks Road if I remember correctly). After the first hour or so I realised the futility of what we were doing because the pay was fourteen dollars per thousand. Before we got in for the third run, my brother, who was twelve at the time, said he'd had enough but Tony insisted we had to finish. We did two more runs of shorter roads and had still only delivered maybe three or four hundred leaflets. At this point Tony was beginning to tire of the experience and he could see our exhaustion very clearly on our red and sweaty faces.

"Get in, that'll do boys." We drove back to his house and realised how many leaflets were still left in the boot. Tony had surreptitiously donated the rest of the leaflets into various local industrial bins and then sat down to calculate how much money we were to get.

"Less the petrol, (it was a big V8 Fairlane) and my time, you get three dollars each". I was incensed and my brother looked at me wide-eyed and said, "Well that was a good idea!" Needless to say neither of us wanted to do that again; but being the fool that I am, I did.

During my studies in Toowoomba I worked several jobs to supplement my meagre student income. Because I was studying Physical Education I thought riding my bike and delivering pamphlets would keep me fit and I suppose it did. Two birds with one stone. The pay was better than my first attempt and I planned it out so that I could cover the most ground in the shortest time. I rigged my bike with a basket at the front and the carrier at the back holding a large cardboard box of pamphlets. I also attached a backpack and front pack loaded with pamphlets for easy access. In this manner I delivered my thousand in an afternoon sometimes up and down steep hills, still peppered by savage dogs and home owners who would scream at me, "Don't you dare dump that shit in my letterbox you little prick or I'll let the dogs at ya!" The thirty odd dollars I got was a bonus above the obvious fitness benefits but I was determined to deliver them all and fulfil my duty properly.

When I told the guy to pay me that afternoon he was suspicious. "Most people take three or four days to do that; you didn't dump them did you? I'm going to check where you went." I assured him they were all delivered and he reluctantly paid me. He did eventually randomly check some of the streets I had delivered to and rang me to see if I wanted to do more even offering to raise the price per pamphlet but I demurred saying I had to concentrate on my studies. It was mostly the savage dogs that turned me off a repeat performance.

Many years later I was driving back from the surf at Moffat Headland when I spotted this teenage boy of about fourteen carrying a huge backpack of pamphlets. He was sneaking into Watson Park and unloading the pamphlets in a huge pile just inside the boundary of trees. I pulled up beside him and wound down the window. He saw me and began frantically picking up the pamphlets and trying to stuff them into his back pack.

"You're not dumping them are you," I asked quietly.

"No, no, they just fell out when I was having a rest."

"Make sure you deliver all of them buddy or you'll never have a clear conscience for the rest of your life." I smiled and drove off seeing him in the rear vision mirror trudging up the road looking back at me as I disappeared around the corner. I'm pretty sure he dumped them somewhere else because I never saw any in my letterbox.

'A social education?'

Another small job I had for one day was helping my friend Dennis O'Hara collect the monthly fee for paper deliveries. We were in grade eight together with a bunch of other Irish boys. He and his dad would deliver the papers and then Dennis would go round to the people who hadn't paid and try to collect the money. I was just his assistant and not really doing much except watching him ask for money. I felt like a twelve year old bouncer but looked too much like a 12yr old girl to have any real effect on the miscreant payers. I was shocked when a lot of people told us to 'fuck off' or claimed they had already paid for it or slammed the door in our faces. It was a thankless job with less than a third willing to pay and some of them only paying a third or less. I only lasted that one day but I did get an insight into people and how they lived because I was interested in their homes. Some of them were complete hovels with unkempt lawns and shit strewn throughout the yards and the houses. Some of them stunk of piss and alcohol and cigarettes (which they could afford) but couldn't scrape up a couple of dollars for the paper boy. I wished Dennis luck on his next round and sprinted home to the relatively tidy and organised abode I called home. I earned fifty cents which was enough for two games of pinball and some lollies at the corner shop.

> 'To see a world in a grain of sand
> and heaven in a wild flower.
> To hold infinity in the palm of your hand
> and eternity in an hour.'
>
> (William Blake)

A skill I learned as a young boy eventually led to a source of income when I really needed it. I had learned from my uncle Peter when we fished at Sunshine Beach. It was definitely a skill that required practice but in a relatively short amount of time I became quite proficient as a result of my 'soft hands'. The gentle touch, patience and concentration were important, as was speed. Sand Worms can sense a pulse in the human thumb and disappear three feet into the sand in a millisecond much to the frustration and exasperation of most people who attempt this very specialized skill. When we fished up at Teewah, the worms were more numerous and somewhat larger and would stretch to over two metres as they were ceremoniously dragged from the sand. They are excellent bait for anything and nowadays only people with a licence are allowed to catch them in certain areas of Queensland and NSW.

In my younger days I used to just catch them for myself or for my grandmother who fished in Weyba Creek for whiting and flathead although any fish could not refuse the lure of a fresh sand worm.

When I moved to Marcus Beach as a nineteen year old, I had

managed to get a job with a catering company that did food for school camps at Camp Cal in Coolum; (another story). The work involved early mornings and late afternoons so I had the whole middle of the day to myself. Usually, if there was good surf, I would surf but on other days my mind turned to obtaining extra money. I saw the worms every time I was on the beach and formulated the idea that I would sell them to the bait shops and boat hire places on the river at Noosaville. I took samples into each of the businesses and, when all three had agreed to pay me twenty cents per worm, I was engaged in worming when the weather and tides were conducive.

My office was a two kilometre stretch of Marcus Beach in one of the most deserted parts of the Sunshine Coast. A few locals and occasional surfers frequented that part of the beach and eventually everyone knew who I was and what I was doing bending over in the sand. "There's that worming guy." I wore a large hat and attached a bucket to a belt around my waist. In a morning I could catch up to four or five hundred (sometimes with both hands) and have them at the bait shop by the late afternoon. I used old fish frames to swish into the incoming waves and lure the worms closer to the stink. In each hand I had a piece of fish flesh or a pippy if I could find one. The O Boats, T Boats and Pelican Boat hire only bought them from me when they had run out so it was not every day. However, the extra income of eighty dollars a batch was enough to pay my weekly rent so I was definitely ahead.

I enjoyed the solitude of the beach with no bosses breathing down my neck and no real deadlines to meet. If I caught enough in the first two days, the worms could be kept alive with some sand

and refrigeration for at least a couple of days. My girlfriend Lily was shocked when she came home one day to find 500 worms squirming around in a large blue Tupperware cake container in the fridge. "That's a hundred bucks of phylum Annelida" I would proudly proclaim. At night I would write sad songs and snippets for stories.

On a recent trip to NSW I went into a bait store to buy worms and realised that they are now $2 each and that the bait shop has to show that they had procured the worms from a licensed dealer. At that rate my daily batch of worms from 1979 would have been worth $800. GULP! I still catch the occasional few for my own purposes or for friends. You can find them anywhere from Bribie to Fraser Island and beyond, if you look close enough.

'Finger lickin' good...'

After my aborted teenage attempts to earn money delivering pamphlets I was still looking for something that would enable me to have my own income which I would usually spend on tuckshop, pinball, lollies or a ten pack of Wild Woodbine smokes (yes I was a smoker at age fourteen). I was in year ten and old enough to be employed. My mother had just got a job at the first ever KFC in Queensland and she actually met Colonel Sanders at the store in Kedron. Wow! She mentioned to the boss, Pat that I was looking for work. I got the job just because I was young and cheap labour but I worked hard. It was always after school and weekends. I lived three doors away so I was easy to call if someone else hadn't come in.

My usual roster was the busy nights, Thursday, Friday and Saturday with an occasional Sunday or cheap Tuesday thrown in. I scrubbed pots vigorously, cut and dusted the chicken ready to be cooked and generally cleaned up around the place mopping floors and rearranging the cold room. It was a hot workplace and some days the patrons were lined up outside the door waiting for a bucket of the newest thing in town; 'Fast Food'. 1975.

Needless to say the floor was covered in slippery grease and they gave us the most inappropriate footwear for the job which was white galoshes. It was like skating with a pot of hot oil in your hand. Ah, the simple days. I bought David Bowie records with my wages.

One of the guys I worked with was a bit older and very good at the dangerous cooking side of things with hot oil and pressure cookers constantly on the go. Dave was very particular about cleaning the pots and making sure the oil was changed as often as possible. I learned a lot from him in a short amount of time and soon enough I was cooking regularly while another younger guy was hired to do what I had been doing.

It wasn't exactly rocket science but there was a definite routine that had to be followed or Pat (the boss) would lose his shit and swear at everyone and everything until it was ship shape. We mixed giant containers of cold coleslaw and potato salad by hand until it was up to our armpits. Potato and gravy and buns had to be heated and crinkle cut chips cooked from the frozen packet. I still remember the smell of my clothes after a few hours in the KFC sweat shop and it was as though every dog, cat and vagrant would follow me home.

At the end of my shifts, which would finish about ten or eleven depending on the night, all my friends would be waiting outside or at my house to get stuck into the barrel of leftovers that I was allowed to bring home. It would disappear quickly and we would also have cold left overs for the next day at school. Despite being popular with my friends I had also started to accumulate some serious money but I was working for it and was often called in to do shifts to replace someone else. During my senior year I was working as sort of an assistant manager on weekends and evenings despite my needing to concentrate on my studies. At the end of the year my academic results were not enough to get me into medicine so I persevered with KFC and eventually found myself as assistant manager at the new store on the corner of Gympie Road and Richmond Rd (it's still there). I was working weekends and nights while my friends were all out socialising and drinking. I would open the store, cook up batches of chicken and all the accoutrement that went with it before the first staff would arrive and occasionally I would close the store and be home by eleven o'clock with a barrel of chicken to share with my drunken mates.

On one occasion, the cook had been cutting chickens up on the electric saw and his hands were frozen from handling the chickens for an hour or so. He came running to me holding his hand with blood spurting out everywhere throughout the back of the store. He had inadvertently grabbed his own thumb instead of the chicken wing and sawed it through.

"I can't find my thumb," he said with a pale, shocked look on his face. I gave him some paper towel to stanch the flow of blood and started rummaging through the bucket of chicken guts below the saw which was still spinning. I felt around in the offal and eventually saw what I thought was a thumb and held it up proudly. Nope, it's a neck. More searching revealed the thumb but Dave had quietly slipped into unconsciousness and was lying on the floor with blood now spurting across the floor and his dirty apron. Everyone else stood back and refused to help.

"Call the ambulance," I yelled at one of the girls on the front counter who was serving. Others were feinting and screaming. I wrapped the thumb in a big towel and tied two rubber bands around it and looked up to see Pat come through the door.

"What's going on here Steve?"

"Matt's cut his thumb off and Sheila is calling the ambulance." He walked over and hung up the phone and sent Sheila back out the front. He told me to sit Matt up and proceeded to slap him around til he emerged from his feint. "Get up," he said almost callously. Matt slowly rose against the wall with my help and looked down at his thumb which was now tucked under the rubber band on the outside of the bloodied towel.

"Drive yourself to the hospital; you'll be fine." He looked at me as if to say 'What?'

"Maybe I should drive him?"

"You're still on duty", he said motioning someone to clean up the mess.

"I'm covered in blood Pat; I can't serve or cook anything." He looked me over and said, "Go home and have a shower and come back." I lived three houses away.

Matt had made his way out to the car park dripping blood all the way and somehow managed to make it to the hospital. When I returned minutes later Pat had restored everything to operating normality. He wasn't even scheduled to be in that day but had dropped in to check on me in my new role as assistant manager. He beckoned me into the small office and leaned in close.

"I don't want any negative things to happen to our store and if you had called the ambulance I would have had to explain to my bosses and the QLD manager what happened. We could lose our jobs over this." He expected me to understand but I was appalled that he would not want an ambulance to come to the store and that he made Matt drive to the hospital. "If he can drive it's not that serious. My brother blew his hand off in a dynamite explosion and he managed to get to the hospital without an ambulance." That was it. He left and we continued running the store as per usual until I closed up and made sure there was no evidence of Matt's blood anywhere. Later that night I wrote a song called 'My bloody thumbs in the chicken guts'. Matt was off for a week and I filled his job.

After a busy weekend, I opened the store on Monday hoping for a usually quiet day and Matt turned up with his thumb bandaged, wiggled it at me, and said that they sewed it back on. I couldn't imagine him being able to handle food for a while but he seemed confident and said that his thumb just felt a bit numb. I rang Pat and he said Matt was 'under no circumstances to work'. I told Matt and he left thinking that he would be back soon enough but after a phone call and a letter from some distant administrator, he was dismissed. I never found out whether he was compensated for his injury (this was 1977 mind you) or whether he regained enough use of his thumb to be employed in any other job that required an opposable thumb but I have been on the lookout for someone with a stitched on right thumb ever since. I too, was eventually sacked, for not having the peas ready before opening time on Saturday. C'est La Vie. I have mixed reactions to the smell of KFC.

'That's entertainment!'

While I was gainfully employed as a teacher I had a call from a friend who asked me if I would host a Trivia Night at the Sunshine Beach Surf Club on Wednesdays. The gig would last over ten weeks and I would be paid a hundred dollars a night. "Sure, sounds like fun."

My wife and I turned up on the first night a bit earlier and had a lovely counter meal and a drink before I would kick the show off with microphone in hand. It had been well advertised and teams were there to win the cartons of beer and bottles of wine. There were minor prizes as well including six packs and food vouchers but it was the prestige of victory which made the teams competitive. I had the questions sent to me by E-mail and I rattled off the categories for the first half to everyone's satisfaction. I then had to collect the team answers and correct or mark them before announcing the progressive scores.

There was one section which required them to listen to music but the club stereo/cd player wasn't working so we skipped that section and ploughed on handing out small prizes for each category. Each week it became more popular and more teams turned up. On the third week I had a visit from a representative of my friends booking agency. He wanted me to sign some forms to register myself with the company and become an official employee but I said 'I didn't want to register this, to have to pay tax and it was only a favour for a friend'. He was insistent and I was recalcitrant, eventually saying, "If you don't want me to do this, get someone else." He reluctantly relented and I continued my Wednesday Trivia nights turning up religiously and completing my task as best I could.

I did eventually get paid and it was a thousand bucks I didn't have before, although I'm sure my wife and I spent more than half of it having dinner and drinks at the club.

'Listen to the music.'

Of the more than forty jobs I was ever paid for, music makes up the most numerous. Although I had lessons at school from Rick Farbach, I wasn't what you would call, a talented musician, so after a few goes at playing the chords to 'Puff the Magic Dragon' I was sort of on my own. I had a guitar, which was great, and I used to pretend I was Jimmy Page or Jimi Hendrix but my skills were well short of those two prodigious talents.

My family had told me that music was not a career that would make money and to concentrate on my school studies, so there was no encouragement or enthusiasm about pursuing this path in life, although my sister and I would make up nonsense songs using the three or four chords I knew and whatever we were looking at at the time, 'The Drapes' 'The The'. Yes, well before the actual band came up with that name. I think my sister spilt the beans and told everyone, before Facebook mind you, about 'The The'. I wrote silly lyrics about 'the biggest tomato in the world' and 'why do all the good bands have 'the' in front of their names?'

A school friend, Tony Tofoni, who used to have the lesson directly after mine, was a natural and gifted musician and over the years, I pestered him to show me jazz chords and other stuff that I thought would be a shortcut to becoming like Jimmy or Jimi. He was very patient and I eventually realised I would have to practice scales and theory which I found quite boring as any kid who's had piano lessons will tell you. I did practice but not furiously like many other teenage boys who would lock themselves in their bedroom for days at a time stripping the bark off their maple guitar necks.

When I was working in Toowoomba many years later, boarding at a house in Rangeville, I was somewhat bored and found a guitar lying around. I roughly tuned it to their out-of-tune piano and bought a Neil Young songbook called 'Harvest'. It had all the chord shapes and lyrics and I knew the songs so I spent many hours in my bedroom trying to sound a bit fluent changing chords. I bought or borrowed other books but as I could not read music I was limited to playing the chord shapes of songs that I already knew. 'Old Man, look at my life'.

When I returned to Brisbane I used to go and see bands in 'The Valley' and would watch them closely thinking that I wanted to eventually do what they were doing but they were all schooled, experienced musicians. I met up with Tony again and started trying to play along with him but once again I was not in his league and never would be. While I was working a 'real' job earning money I would play and practice at night when I could. I had some singing lessons and finally belted out my first complete song which was Cat Steven's 'Father and Son'; still one of my favourites. I'd also learned, 'You're No Good,' by Linda Ronstadt. My singing teacher bravely suggested I sing 'Life on Mars' which I eventually massaged into a massacre. Sorry David.

An opportunity arose when a new (Start-up?) band was looking for a singer and I went along to audition. I don't remember what we played but they must have thought that I could pull it off (or no one else turned up) so they asked me to come to rehearsal and gave me a list of songs which I knew very little of at the time. Thus, was formed, 'Thirteen O'clock'; a tragic name and just as tragic a band when I think about it. We played Chuck Berry and Roy Orbison and Elvis and it was very 50's Rock 'n' Roll with a few more modern songs thrown in ('Breaking us in Two' by Joe Jackson and 'Land Down Under' by 'Men at Work' with David Brownstein, the bass player, playing the flute part). We also played Johnny Diesel's song '8675309'. It wasn't my preferred listening music but I persevered and we got gigs through an agent. The rhythm guitarist, Michael, was one of those typically Skunk Baxter (think Muppets band) looking dudes with the long hair and handlebar moustache.

He wore tight pants and his gigantic balls slid down each leg of his flares outlining all the rest of him to anyone who wished to look and also to anyone who didn't. The lead guitarist looked like Bingo from the Banana Splits.

Yes, just picture that character for a minute and add a big semi-acoustic Gibson guitar. He loved his music and knew all the riffs for all the songs although not always in time, as he'd get excited and speed up for a bit and then relent when we all stared at him and he heard the rhythm section kick in again. He would give a big Bingo smile and continue.

The bass player had straight blonde hair in a Beatles cut and I suspected he was Jewish with a name like David Brownstein. He was quite a good musician and played flute and piano as well as bass and could sing a harmony if required. Twenty-one year old Steve Foy ended up being our drummer after an enthusiastic 17 year old had tried to tell us that 'he was good; mum said so' and 'all the good band names are gone. Imagine if we could get the name 'The Rolling Stones.' We rolled our eyes and sent him back to the supermarket packing section. We had a uniform which consisted of white shirts and a black thin tie and sunglasses (ironically, the band I am playing in at the moment has the exact same outfit but we play Ska). We were playing at the Queens Hotel one night when the drummer accidently locked himself inside the green room after we'd had a smoke and it took a full half an hour before the manager arrived and unlocked the door. The residual smoke from the joint fumed out and Steve staggered onto the stage. The manager pointed out that the door was locked from the inside. Good one Steve. We did get another gig there despite the terrible sound system and the cheap pay.

We got gigs in The Orient Hotel and other inner city venues and suburban pubs. We did parties and weddings and filled in for more famous bands like 'Wickety Wak' who'd double booked themselves one night. The crowd that turned up that night at the Ferny Grove Tavern to see 'Wickety Wak' was, to say the least, disappointed at our mostly unrehearsed renditions of songs but they were already there and half pissed and we played til eleven o'clock getting most people up to dance. Lots of family and friends were there to support us. Thank you all.

I had earned money as a musician (the same amount I earn now as a musician; ha!) but was still super-self-critical of my performances on most occasions. Sometimes I would play a bit of guitar but mostly I was the front guy trying to relate to the audience and announcing each song before we played it just in case they couldn't work out what it was.

I wrote and recorded songs with David Brownstein in 'Big Balls Michaels' garage and eventually, when we all drifted apart, the tapes had been lost to the world forever. I suspected David had a copy of them and I swear I heard one on the radio many years later.

Since then I have played with many different people, recorded albums of my own songs at my own expense and written songs for other people. Tony was always a constant in all of these bands (except thirteen o'clock) and was instrumental (pun) in making all our recordings sound professional and unique.

Tony and I played mostly jazz rock and blues with a sax player named Kenny Bradshaw but did also venture into other genres depending on who we were playing with at the time. Me and Tony have played lots of venues on the Sunshine Coast, Brisbane, The Gold Coast and festivals including a recent Woodford Folk Festival (with the Ska band), all of which earned me money albeit not enough to become even a thousandaire.

I could probably write another book about all the intricacies of our music world because it was humorous at times but always enjoyable, from my point of view at least. I feel I should highlight some of the more memorable gigs we played and stick more expediently to the jobs side of this story. Don't mind my little side indulgence.

In 2000 I was asked to play at the opening of the Kings Beach amphitheatre for the 'Mountains to the Sea Festival'. We had just recorded our first album and we had played the songs live for a few months beforehand so we were reasonably rehearsed. It was a huge event with thousands of people filling the park and spilling over from the Pearl Hotel. Our slot was between a Beatles cover band complete with Sergeant Pepper outfits and the main act, Venetta Fields. Wow!

We were feeling a bit out of our depth for sure because Venetta had recorded with our favourite band, Steely Dan and we were in awe of her. I spoke to her briefly asking about her recording with 'The Dan' and she said she had never met them and recorded her bits somewhere else. We walked on stage to a great introduction from a lovely local radio announcer, "Ladies and Gentlemen, please welcome our own local band performing here today, 'Ipso Facto'. Let me just take you back twenty four hours before this.

Our very experienced drummer (ask me about this guy sometime) for the recording and live gigs up to this point was of a certain religious bent and the night before we were due to play, he rang me and said that his elders had told him he couldn't play because they may be singing the national anthem on that day. I was incredulous. "Are you shitting me?" I asked, expecting him to say he was only joking. He wasn't and hung up. I looked at Kenny with dread in my eyes and explained the dilemma. Within minutes he had procured a proficient drummer in Joel Finnegan and we rehearsed all the songs the morning before we played. He nailed it even though he had not ever played our songs live. Good on you Joel Finnegan!

Back to the stage on the day; we did a quick line check and

I welcomed the crowd including all my friends who were whooping it up at the pub. We played our set with what I thought was consummate professionalism and although the songs were mostly original, everyone applauded and whistled. With the new drummer Joel slotting right in with me on the bass and Tony on guitar we belted out a good forty minute set. Kenny Bradshaw played his beloved mark four sax, with bulging veins in his forehead, like it was his last moment on earth. He was married to it and still is. The song 'Der Grosse Welt' was made for that day.

Andy, who had done our recording, played some wonderfully trippy keys on 'Void' and Derek Meyers was the other brilliant and naturally talented guitarist swapping solos with Tony throughout. (See Escher's Crystal Ball and Void on our first album.)

At one point before we played 'Slimpick', I asked if there was anyone in the audience who could play harmonica. Some guy down the front called out and held up his harp which happened to be in the same key as the song we were about to play. It was of course pre-arranged with my friend Simon Norman. He was on the recording of the song and came up to play it with us. He wore his usual boardies, Ramones T-shirt and double plugger thongs. It went off famously and we were cheered and applauded which was the biggest event most of us had ever played. 'Give me no money, give me no fame'… we were paid $300 for that gig.

In the side tent afterwards Venetta congratulated us and was about to go on as the headliner. I stopped her and said, "There's a bit of lipstick on your teeth Venetta." She thanked me and turned to her mother who wiped it off with a tissue as she headed up the stairs to sing like an angel. We were all on a high and proceeded to get really pissed for the rest of the afternoon and evening. It took me days to get over that experience with adrenaline rushes every time I thought about it. I never would have thought that when I was playing Puff the Magic Dragon at school that I would be playing on a stage like that to three thousand people. Or maybe I did?

I never felt that I pursued music as a career but it somehow pursued me for its own mystical purposes. I just fell into a lot of things over the years and they always seemed to work whether it was me at the front or me just playing as part of the band. I will admit that I was the motivator in many instances when other musicians felt that it was an impossible task. I booked gigs and set up the PA and humped amps and stands and mics all over the place but it was never a chore once you started that first song and everyone played as a group and not as individuals because in music that will never work. I learnt my best chops by playing with better musicians. Thanks to all those musos by the way.

Tony and I played lots of odd gigs but the one at the Moffat Beach newsagency to promote the launch of my new book (another job) was memorable as we sat on milk crates at the front of the store, played our original songs and when someone wanted to buy a book I would go inside and sign it for them. The usual Saturday morning crowd who were going about their business milled around the newsagency to see this novelty of the entertainment world. My mum and sister were there cajoling people to buy the books. Thank you.

We had also played with a band called Bohemian Rogue which consisted of Clive Carter singing and playing guitar, Tony was doing the noodly bits on his Gibson Lucille, Giovanna on bass and Pete playing mandolin. What was I doing you may well ask? ; playing the drums. Yes, I had become an accidental drummer and sang some back up bits for Clive's well-crafted and catchy tunes. We played local gigs for a year or so, recorded an album of his songs and Clive's music career was reborn. Because I was busy playing bass with The Sunny Coast Rude Boys and working on another album with Tony, my time was a bit precious and I opted to leave the Rogues. Tony agreed that he too would step down at that point and Pete got on the bandwagon saying he didn't think he felt professional enough to be playing live. Clive and Gio continued to play with Gary who is a great mandolin player but Gio left and so it's down to two and they are doing wonderfully as a duo. 'Go Clive'; Tamworth awaits your talents.

A month or so after the Bohemian Rogue schism, Clive approached us and asked if Tony and I would play one of his songs with him at the J at Noosa. It was a 'Songs of Summer' competition (which we performed in winter) and Clive had already written 'Ode to Moffs' which fitted the requirements perfectly. Twelve artists and bands performed on the night, some internationals, some very polished local musicians (who put together a super band for the night) and local bands from Coolum and Byron Bay; and us... Everyone played one song and the judges from Noosa Radio would pick the song they thought reflected the Sunny Coast and summer. My performance on the drums was rather sub-standard and Tony missed his cue for the solo, which is very unlike him, but we nursed it through to its final bars and received a full-hearted applause. 'I think Stephen lost his car keys...'

I rushed offstage apologising for my sloppy playing but Clive seemed in a good mood and was happy to have played the J. As the last few acts were playing their one song to summarise summer, we were in the auditorium watching the young guns pounding out a metalish song which was very well played and we sort of assumed that there were a lot of better musicians playing that night. It didn't matter. They announced third place and then second and then with a resounding audience support to the decision, 'Bohemian Rogue' had won the thousand dollar prize and the prestige of having the song played on local radio for the next year or so. Clive was out of his skin with excitement and as he accepted the award he gave a special mention to me as his motivation to get his songs out there. I was very touched by his humble honesty. Thanks Clive.

I had encouraged him to sing live, and watched, as all his doubts about playing to a real audience flew out the window. That was another job I got paid for although I hadn't expected it really. I was just happy to be playing music. Clive's songs are great by the way; look up 'Bohemian Rogue'. (Insert gratuitous cross-media plug here)

More recently, as bass player for the **'Sunny Coast Rude Boys'**, I have earned a little pocket money playing at festivals and support gigs for internationals and touring bands such as 'Bad Manners' and 'The Original Wailers'. We have released three songs which I co-wrote with Tony and Mick Hughes, **'Way Down'**, **'Rude Style'** and **'El Rollo'** which recently hit the number eleven spot in Beefy's Ska top 30.; Google, Spotify, YouTube us and have a look.

When I was watching bands in the valley in the eighties I would see musicians who I thought were brilliant and aspired to play with people like that including Tony, Mick Donnelly and Laurie Telford who had been playing in different bands for years.

Twenty-five years later I was asked to play a 50th birthday party for a local guy called Martin who had seen me playing at a party up the coast with Glen Poulton on guitar and Mad Dan Higgins deftly animating his drum kit into a thunderstorm. I told Martin that it would not be the same line up except for me and he insisted on me and whoever playing his party at his house in Windsor. I asked Tony if he could get Laurie and Michael for the gig and they agreed. I think we had one rehearsal before everyone was ofay to play. I realised, during one of the ripping guitar solos at the party that night, that here I was playing with those guys I used to idolise years before and thought, 'I can't be that bad a musician after all'. We were paid six hundred dollars. Thankyou Mick Donnelly and Laurie Telford; Who'd have thought Tony and I would be playing Woodford Folk Festival ten years later with the Rudeez.

I was recently offered a job at a new club in town for six hundred dollars and immediately thought of Tony, Mick and Laurie to complete the line-up but it was too short a notice for everyone and we have postponed til later in the year (covid). The repertoire would have been almost identical to the one we played at Martin's party ten years earlier; which goes to show that some music is timeless, and musicians get paid eighties wages.

I met Eric Burdon backstage after his performance with the Young Animals at the Civic Centre in Caloundra. He put sunnies on for the photos and I said "You don't need them." He pulled his bottom eyelid down, looked at me and said, "There's a lot of rock and roll in there." For a seventy-something year old, his performance was flawless and he sang a David Bowie song in tribute to the great 'star man' who had recently returned to his original planet in space. I am a big fan of Bowie and his music has influenced much of my song writing.

Paul Kelly was performing in a show in Brisbane to commemorate the Irish history of Australia. Mick and I went back stage to meet the cast. Shane Howard was standing next to Paul as I approached them and introduced myself. "Paul, we are doing one of your songs as a Ska version, I hope you don't mind."

"Which one?" he asked.

"Dumb Things," I said sheepishly.

He thought for a minute and then said, "Yeh, that'll work." We got the nod and have played it ever since, although the story of how it came about has been lavishly elaborated upon when explained to any of our audiences. Perhaps Paul will sing it with us one day?

We have played with or supported artists such as Lior, The Lyrical, (our first official gig at The Shared in Yandina), Sahara Beck (who supported us when starting out, again at The Shared), Nicky Bomba, The Tooth Faeries, Melbourne Ska Orchestra, Pat Powell, Strange Tenants and various reggae bands at the

International Ska Festival and Island Vibe on Stradbroke Island. The 'Blues on Broadbeach' gig was one of my most memorable festival crowds. Thanks Mick H.

I had some interesting conversations with Wally De Backer at the original Sol Bar in Coolum when he started 'The Basics' (Kenny played sax with them that night at my insistence) and again at Caloundra music festival, playing with the 'The Basics'. The rest of the festival I got pissed watching the Rugby League Grand Final with Glen Wheatley. I introduced Mark Moroney to him and gave him one of Mark's CD's.

Now, I'm just name-dropping I know, but music took me in this direction and most of the time I wasn't really looking to 'hook up with the rich and famous' of the music world. They just happened to be where I was at the time and I am not backwards in coming forwards to say hello to anyone; ask my wife.

I had earned money playing music and am still playing just for the fun of it, but perhaps, in the back of my mind, hoping that someone more astute or desperate in the music world will hear one of my songs and want to record it.

I often said to Tony, the ultimate tribute would be to hear your songs being played in an elevator or shopping centre on 'muzak'.

If I quoted every gig I was paid for, I would be well over the forty jobs mark by now so I'm only going to attribute ten to the total. The most I've been paid for a gig per person was $200.00, but the experience of playing live and the riders are infinitely more valuable.

'I wasn't charming enough to be a convincing bullshitter....'

At certain points in my life I was willing to try anything to earn money. The ads stated 'Earn good money' and they'd quote a ridiculous figure; 'be your own boss', 'guaranteed clientele', 'must be friendly and outgoing'. Ok, I'll bite, what is it?

I went to an interview (dressed appropriately with business shirt and tie) which consisted of twenty or so people sitting in a room listening to the top salesman enthusiastically sprout his monetary conquests in this market. He then proceeded to demonstrate how he would sell the 'pots n pans' using some of the applicants as guinea pigs in the presentation. They were stainless steel, copper-lined pots with a lifetime guarantee and a huge range of choices. I was convinced they were good. He then went into the second phase of the sale, if there wasn't too much enthusiasm for his original product, he revealed a bone china set of crockery as a bonus if you purchased the pots and pans. "Look how tough they are; that's ash china." He would then proceed to put a dinner plate upside down on the floor and stand on it just to prove its strength although I suspected it was something to do with the shape of the plate and physics. Then he came to the 'piece de resistance' when all else failed to make a sale; 'The Steak Knives'. Beautifully crafted Westminster steel (or whatever other English county he could think of but missed Wiltshire) serrated, with comfortable wooden handles and ergonomic balance. I was sold.

If the client bought the entire set of pots and pans for fourteen hundred dollars that was fine but if they didn't bite the first time the crockery would be thrown in; if not, the knives would come out. They still got all the pots and pans, the crockery and the knives for fourteen hundred. Needless to say, my attempts at getting a party of women together to present my demonstration was not easy and my girlfriend's family took pity on me as I did my first pots and pans sale gig. It was a room full of Italian women of varying ages from Nona's to Zia's and their daughters and granddaughters. They knew what they wanted and they didn't want the entire set of pots, they just wanted a few items and I had to explain that it was the package or nothing. They insisted on just certain pots so I relented.

In my frustration when I returned to the office on Monday to see who was on the leader board this week I was nowhere to be seen. Some people had posted seven sales and they had the gross figure of $9600 after their name but their real income was fourteen percent of that so the top sales person (the guy who had demonstrated at the interview) had earned $1344.00 for the week. In those days most people were lucky to earn $300.00 per week in a nine to five so that was an indecent amount. I wanted to find out how he did it and so approached him for some tips.

"What is it Steve? How'd your week go?" He was dressed in his best pink shirt and maroon tie with tailored trousers and very uncomfortable looking shoes. The 'Blue Stratos' after-shave was a little thick as was the aerosol deodorant. His hair was recently cut and streaked and he was pretending to be important by collating and stapling pieces of paper.

"I have a client who just wants certain pots but not all of them because she already has some."

"It's all or nothing Steve, no splitting up sets, how would we sell them afterwards?"

"Ok, I'll put it to them and see what happens? Can I reduce the price a bit because its family?" He nodded his head from side to side for a minute and then said,

"Alright, nine hundred for all the pots and you still get 14% of that for your first sale Steve. What do you think?" I nodded, thought about my $126.00 for a sale and then decided to ask about his record breaking sales for last week. He stood up from his very important desk and walked to the door looking out into the corridor suspiciously and then closed the door gesturing for me to sit down.

He returned to his power chair and leaned back making a little steeple with his fingers while staring out the window at the brick wall next door.

"Steve, I don't usually share my sales secrets with anyone," he looked at me with one of those 'Blue Steel, I'm important and have lots of chicks and money' looks. I nearly guffawed loudly but composed myself to hear his secret.

"What you need to do is think of this as a numbers game. The more people you present to at any one time gives you better odds for a sale. As you know, we have a payment plan, so people who can't immediately afford to pay for the goods can pay them off.

Every woman dreams of a beautiful set of copper-lined stainless steel pots and pans, a dinner set to complete their kitchen and of course, the best steak knives to present to their friends and family." He was still staring out the window as I listened. He sat up suddenly and leaned over to me with his hands clasped together and spoke in low tones.

"Go where there are lots of women working, factories, warehouses, office buildings and ask the manager if you can do a lunchtime or after work presentation. I usually offer something for the boss of course; steak knives or a fifty for his trouble. If they say no, I leave brochures on the lunch table asking anyone who wants to organise a party at their house and offer them a free set of crockery for their efforts. I get a lot like that. They'll organise a group of women to come round and while we're there, other women want to have a party and get free crockery. Of course, you have to make a few sales to compensate for the giveaways but, as I said, it's a numbers game Steve." He looked at me as though I already owed him my life. I thanked him and went to conquer the pots and pans sales world to proudly have my name up on the board next week. In reality, it's a lot harder than that unless you're an experienced bullshitter as I discovered the hard way.

My next gig was another family affair as my brother's girlfriend and her family and friends came to watch the demonstration. I'd offered the steak knives to whoever was hosting. I dragged in my two large suitcases and set up. I did my banter accurately and revealed the pots gradually, handing them to people in the crowd. My 'standing on the plate' act drew 'oohs and ahhs' but no one seemed overly keen to jump up for a purchase.

Although I had answered all their questions and assured them of the lifetime guarantee on the pots and the authenticity of the crockery, I was no nearer to sealing a deal. One of them called out...

"What about the steak knives?' That was supposed to be my clincher but she had pre-empted it as she had seen this pitch before at another party.

"Ok," I said. "These knives are Wiltshire steel, serrated and of the highest quality. If anyone makes a purchase on the pots and pans they will also get the crockery and the knives for free."

"Can we just buy the knives?"

"Can I just have the big pots?"

"No, I want the crockery, it's beautiful."

"What about the knives and two pots?"

This wasn't the way it was supposed to go. I spent the next fifteen minutes pointing out that it was a package of all the pots etc. etc. and putting out fires with individuals who asked about payment plans just for the crockery. In the end there was no sale and I had to hand over the steak knives to the woman who had organised the party. She looked at me as if to say, 'that was easy, thanks; you didn't make a sale you idiot' and smiled as though she had conquered the lotto numbers in one fell swoop. I packed up my wares and drove home rather despondent. I wasn't cut out for this; there was too much bullshitting for me to feel comfortable about this being a way to make a living.

I did visit warehouses and factories and offices only to be told in no uncertain terms to 'fuck off'. There was lots of driving, lots of refusals, which get to you after a while, and no money. It was a hard way to make ends meet. My total income selling pots and pans was a mere $300.00.

'Like flogging a dead horse.'

With my newly gained sales experience, I tried to sell 'Cashcard' for a while (remember that?) The concept went like this. I walked into a local Chinese restaurant (or any other retail business) and said if they displayed the 'Cashcard' sticker in their window, more people would come to the restaurant and present their own personal 'Cashcard' and receive a ten percent discount.

Amazingly, some people signed up but it was again a numbers game and the commission I was earning was pitiful for the amount of time I put in. Hard bullshitting yakka which I felt demeaned me somehow. I didn't believe it would take off, but that's all I had to pay for petrol and beer and food.

Needless to say, I didn't last long in the direct sales world but I kept looking. Total Cashcard income was about $500.00.

'Keep smiling until it hurts.'

I did some TV commercials with a friend of mine from school. Golden Circle was advertising soft drinks and we spent a day on the Southport Broadwater on a boat filming a bunch of us young people cavorting, skiing behind the boat and drinking warm soft drink which they sprayed with water on the can to make it look cold. We ate pineapple and watermelon and did five or six takes of the shot including a close up of me and a girl, Caroline, drinking warm lemonade and trying to make it look refreshing. It was a good day and we received about three hundred dollars each. A few weeks later I walked into a friends place for a visit and his older brother said, "I just saw you on TV." I hadn't seen the ad yet but when I finally did at home with my whole family yelling, 'it's on, it's on' I saw the tail end with the close up of me and Caroline and thought, "Is that me?" Through the same agency, I got gigs promoting different products by dressing up like a grid iron player and running rampant through Queen Street mall throwing the ball to two other similarly dressed guys while the scantily clad cheerleaders handed out brochures and giveaways. The jobs were few and far between and we usually received $60-100 each. I went for lots of auditions but wasn't always 'what they were looking for'. I saw some of the ads eventually and recognised the people who had auditioned. I got call backs for some but got pipped at the post because they were taller or better looking or great actors?

I was usually just trying to ham it up and take the piss but I soon realised they wanted serious all the time, or at least when the director wanted it to be happy or serious.

One audition was for the opening of the Jupiter's Casino on the Gold Coast and there were fifty or more people trying for several different parts. One was in speedos on the beach beside a bikini clad girl, one in the casino and one just frolicking with a girl. The speedos one included six or seven of us standing in front of the director and he looked at all the punters to see who would fit. The guy to my right who had the vertical black and white stripes on his budgie smugglers looked like he had shoved a Cavendish banana down his pants and the director was very quick to dismiss the rest of us. The casino scene used three of us; a girl behind the bar, me as the punter who just won big and another guy pretending to be the pianist. I sort of worked out the scenario for this scene with the other two while we were waiting to be called and they agreed.

When we got up and they told us what the scene was I skipped to the imaginary bar and leaned on it saying, I've just won big at the craps table; my shout; watermelon daiquiris for everyone." The girl behind the bar pretended to make them and the director said, "No! What's with the watermelon daiquiris? Do it again!"

Take two; "I've just won the Keno jackpot; my shout; pineapple daiquiris for everyone."

"No! What's with the fuckin daiquiris? Champagne for fuck's sake." We had a third go but it didn't have the same impact as daiquiris. When I saw the eventual ad on TV there were two couples celebrating at the bar and they were drinking what suspiciously looked like daiquiris. The girl who had played the bar attendant with me was behind the bar and the guy I set up as the fake piano player was the piano player with black suit and bowtie.

The third scene for the casino ad was the young couple walking through Surfers Paradise like two lovers. All the potentials had to pair up and after all the professional advertisement actors had aligned themselves with the perfect guy or girl with the perfect height I had no choice but to approach the only girl left and I was the only guy. In those days, they wanted symmetry so when I approached the 6'1" Chinese girl she couldn't have looked more disappointed but I was more than happy to lead her onto the stage and pretend we were a young couple enjoying the charms of Cavill Avenue on the Gold Coast. When we finished I thanked her and she said 'you too'. The actual ad that aired showed a blonde girl with Farah Fawcett looks and hair and a tall blonde guy with a massive set of teeth, shirtless, running up the beach in their eighties beach wear. I would have preferred the image of me and the tall Chinese girl running up the beach with daiquiris in our hands; a long shot in any casino.

> 'There are only three types
> of people in the world:
> Those who can count
> and those who can't.'

Australian Guarantee Corporation (AGC) was looking for a collections officer. I had no idea what this was but I managed to get to an interview reasonably dressed and was asked what I thought the national anthem should be. I said I liked Waltzing Matilda because it was very Australian. And what do you like to drink? I replied that I enjoyed a cold beer on a hot day. Do you play sport Steve? Yes, I surf, swim, play touch footy. Welcome to AGC Steve and he shook my hand. "Alan will show you the ropes, good luck." I didn't even know what the pay was till the end of the week, (we used to get cash in a packet in those days too with all the coins making it feel heavier.)

Alan led me to a desk amongst dozens of other people at desks and they were all on the phone. My accounts were from L to P which was quite a large file. My job was to ring up people who hadn't paid their loan or lease on a vehicle or other equipment purchased under a commercial leasing arrangement with AGC and convince them to pay or else. There were varying degrees of 'or else'. The interest rates at the time were exorbitant and many people defaulted having to surrender their car and pay for 'recovery' costs. Larger companies were given more leeway if they had hundreds of thousands invested. It was just a constant conversation trying to be calm and friendly but at the same time demanding to have payments made by a certain date. I spoke to thousands of struggling Australians.

We had to achieve percentage targets each week to show we had made progress. For example, in my ledger, I had reduced the number of defaulters to 2.7% (from 4.5% of the previous officer) which was well under the 3.5% minimum required to keep your job. Some people would stay late into the night to catch people at home and make theirs the best figures in the office thereby giving them a distinct advantage for promotion if it came about. I was never really that ambitious and was happy to do my job and go home.

I met some interesting people at AGC including other staff and clients. There were a few women and girls working there and I was keen on a redhead who sat way down the back. She was quiet and rarely spoke to anyone but I liked her green eyes and freckly complexion.

I would occasionally talk to her at the social events upstairs on Friday nights when we would play ping pong, get pissed and then drive home. I did that too many times and eventually paid for it; twice.

I worked in Alan's team. He was 6'1" with black curly hair and he sported a great big black caterpillar moustache and matching eyebrows which did most of his talking for him. He loved his sport and was a champion left hand fast bowler who took 6 for 11 against another finance company we used to play. He was a serious sort of guy but we got on well. He owned a couple of laundromats that we would raid on occasions to get beer money when we were in a taxi going somewhere to have a drink. One night he pissed himself just before he got in the taxi, looked at me and said, 'Yeah, I don't fucking care Ste that was the best piss I've ever had.'

Yee (only part of his name) was Chinese and told me stories of his Kung Fu training which was quite fascinating considering he was training his sons from the age of two. He once demonstrated kicking the coolite tiles out of the ceiling from a standing jump in front of about three or four of us. Someone said, "Fuck Yee, have a beer and relax; you know we can all kick your arse." Yee laughed like a schoolgirl hiding his teeth behind his hands and cracked another beer. He was just one of the boys again.

The telephonist was a large older fake blonde woman with a loud mouth and crass sense of humour. She would often make sexist comments to the young men in the office who took it as it was intended, a joke. She suggested to Phil the salesman, who was surely an alcoholic, to organise a donkey dick competition to see who had the biggest. Phil was sure it was him. He went round the office and asked who wanted to compete. There was a secret betting pool and the 'donkey dick' winner got some of the prize money. Eventually, there was a 'dick off' in the upstairs room and Phil comes down cursing and blaming the air conditioning. Behind him was Peter with a big smile on his face and sixty bucks in his hand. The receptionist thereafter called Pete 'donkey' but he was non-plussed about it and just grinned.

Some lunchtimes we would go across the road to the licensed Chinese restaurant and I was thinking we were going to eat but it was a 'slam beers down as quickly as you can' session even though I did order something to eat. I hardly had time to eat any of the food in order to keep up with Phil and Peter's shout. I realised that the world of finance also included lots of drinking, in and out of office hours.

They set me up several times. I came back from lunch one day with a note on my desk to ring someone. Ok, I rang the number and the woman said Department of Fisheries or something. I politely said, 'Can I speak to Barry Mundi please?" The woman laughed and said, no honey, you've been set up there's no one here by that name. The laughs from around the office gave it away as I realised what I had done; it was a harmless but brutal initiation into the banal humour that tried to detract us from the tedium of low finance.

Another client on my books was a real underground figure who had spent time in jail and was at one point a target of the Fitzgerald inquiry. He was found under his bed hiding with suitcases full of drugs and money and did a couple of years. He owed money on several loans and I had rung him many times threatening legal action if he didn't cough up. He always referred to me as 'you little prick' in the most sanctimonious tones. One day he showed up at the office at Chermside with a briefcase and asked if we could sit in one of the offices. Alan knew who he was and warned me to be careful. "Do you want me to come in with you Ste?" as he called me. "No I'll be fine." I left the door of the office open to be on the safe side and Alan stood outside listening.

"Listen you little prick, do you know who I am?" I looked at his file and said, "It says here your name is Jeffrey." He squirmed and gritted his teeth like he was coming down from some monumental bender and proceeded to open his briefcase. I had given him a figure of about ten thousand that he should pay so that we would not proceed with legal action. He pulled a cheque book out and scribbled something illegible on it. I had been warned that his cheques bounced and suggested he go to the bank across the road and cash it. He spun his suitcase around and I saw the handgun. He tapped it with his finger and said, "Perhaps you'd reconsider taking this cheque" and threw it at me. He waited to see if I would push the envelope.

"Sure, thanks Jeffrey, this'll do fine." He slammed the case shut and strutted out of the room in a huff not looking at anyone else in the building and kicked the door open while saying, "Fuckin pricks!"

Alan looked around the doorway at me and said, "Did he pull the gun on you?"

"Not quite, he just showed it to me in his case, wrote the cheque and left." I was surprisingly calm but later when we were having drinks upstairs some of the guys said that it looked like Jeffrey was wired and could have done anything, being in such a desperate situation. The big boss found out and asked me if I was willing to testify that he had brought a gun into the office, if it came to that, but Jeffrey was his own worst enemy and it never got to that point as he was caught importing large amounts of cocaine. Of course, he would be out of prison by now but I doubt that he would remember the name of the little prick that pissed him off so much that day. Judging by his age at the time and the pastiness of his skin, I'd say he would not be alive.

After eight months or so in Chermside, Alan came to me with a proposition to go uptown into the central commercial leasing department. He had heard of the job through a mate and had faith in me to join him as his office 'Johnny' while he went out on the road selling or 'repping' as they called it then. Apparently, Alan thought I had a good phone manner.

At first I was hesitant because this Chermside job was ten minutes' drive from home and the new one would be in town, which meant public transport and dressing up a bit and carrying some kind of fake leather valise. We both got the job probably at Alan's insistence that I be part of his team. I was touted as a bit of a whizz-kid with the books as I'd consistently achieved good percentages at Chermside, although, I wasn't the best.

> 'Everyone is born with a blank slate
> and all the people you meet
> write on your slate.'
>
> (John Locke)

This job at AGC central leasing was different. This was a different hierarchy of sucking up and office dynamics. Everyone was trying to look good and dominate everyone else. It was a typical eighties scene with Styrofoam coffee cups filled with the most disgusting International dogshit, powdered milk and white sugar or saccharin. Everyone seemed to have the same Paul Young or Sting haircuts with streaks (except Mike who wore his dad's old toupee because he couldn't afford to fork out for a new one and didn't want to accept his baldness yet) and pretended to be more important than they really were. Most people didn't know what they were supposed to be doing but the management had a lot of long lunch meetings. Mullets, in varying forms, were also popular amongst those who wanted to spend more than ten bucks for a haircut and go disco dancing like John Travolta. Alan and I and his other salesmen had more generic homogenised hairstyles often done cheaply at a local barber. We had boring fashion sense but as Alan said, 'We're not show ponies Ste.'

The aftershave and deodorant smells as you walked out of the elevator to the seventh floor were enough to give you an olfactory headache. The girls were just as bad but made sure they wafted those scents in the right direction. Blue eyelids and bright lipstick worked magic in a job once you had wafted your expensive NO.5 in the right direction and wore the right high heels and haircut. Air conditioning didn't do much for your skin in those days and the fluoro lights sort of flickered unnaturally through the whole floor which was barren and unwelcoming to say the least.

My immediate boss Mike, who was not that much older than me, and a complete dickhead, wore an obvious and badly fitted toupee and drank lots of coffee while looking over my shoulder with one hand in his pocket. I don't think he really knew what he was supposed to be doing so he harassed Graham (my Chinese offsider) and then made lurid comments to our dedicated but quite unattractive secretary. She was way too thin, never smiled and never engaged with anyone by her own choice. There was a constant look of serious terror on her face. Sometimes she would magically appear beside my desk and I would jump.

She was apparently quite efficient at her job but someone nudged me at the water cooler one day and said, "When are you going to take her down to the car park?" Apparently most of the shallow and fatuous men in the office including the big boss had at some point taken her down to the car park for 'lunch'. I showed the guy a picture of my girlfriend at the time and he said, "Yeah, but you know, why not?" I stood looking at him incredulously.

No wonder I didn't get on well with most of these creatures. They were Neanderthals.

The only people I really spent any time with were moustache Alan; the other salesman named Alan who was a short ginger-haired man who shared the same surname as the moustached Alan, and my close colleague at the time, Graham, whose family owned a large catering company.

I found out soon enough that my immediate boss, Mike, got the job by being the big boss's tennis coach. All makes sense now. Graham relied on me to help him with his accounts and how to speak to people on the phone because his accent and slight stutter tended to be an obstacle for him. He spent many overtime hours getting his chops in the finance industry which I guessed he would eventually transfer into his own family catering business.

One of my accounts was a huge commercial leasing account on plant and equipment owned by the Main Roads Minister at the time (yes, the same one from the Brisbane Club) . He was overdue lots and we were going to repossess his Jaguar and some of his bulldozers. Every time I rang I would talk to his wife who was lovely. She would apologise and say that she needed the Jag and would deposit some money the next day. All the other accounts were allowed to run over somewhat despite my earnest efforts to bring them to legal conclusions and write off the rest of the loan. The big boss called me to his office one day and said, "Leave those accounts to me." It was obviously political. That was it. I backed off. My figures didn't look good after a month or so because those accounts were worth millions.

Remember the efficient secretary I mentioned. I never really gave her anything more than a polite hello. I had been asked to pull a major account and send statements to the proprietors (way before E-mails). Once they were collated I gave them to her and she asked if it was this company or that. There were two very similar names. I gave her the correct one. She had then apparently mailed them to the other company and blamed me when the shit hit the fan. Apparently, she was a more valuable asset to the company than I. The big boss called me in Monday and I was sacked despite the fact that I had Graham to witness my statements. Oooh! Was it because I hadn't taken my secretary to 'lunch' or because my immediate boss, Mike, was a pain in the arse and that Graham and I were doing a lot of his work for him? I was trying to justify myself but to no avail. I remained calm and breathed.

Either way, I was the scape-goat who had to be made an example of so the big clients knew that the company was serious. I smiled and sarcastically thanked the 'big boss' for my brief employment. Somehow, I felt a kind of relief because I really didn't fit into this world of arse-licking, power-dressing and cheap coffee; not to mention the lurid chauvinistic innuendos that peppered their water-cooler conversations. It was a cultural and intellectual desert. I wasn't cut out for the cut-throat world of high finance; or was it low finance?

As I walked back to my desk and collected my stuff Graham asked me what it was about.

"They sacked me." I didn't explain why, because stilted secretary and Toupee Mike were sitting within earshot behind us. I shook Graham's hand and said that it had been good working with him. He looked puzzled and looked back at Mike who was watching. Mike had a leer on his face which showed that he was somewhat satisfied with my dismissal. I walked towards the elevator and was caught by the three salesmen, Alan, Alan and an older guy who had just left of his own accord called, you guessed it, Alan.

"What's up Ste?" moustached Alan asked, like David Caruso in CSI. I explained briefly while the elevator was making its way up to the seventh floor. The other Alans shook their heads with disgust and the older one said, "You know Steve; sometimes you just have to go out there and get your hands dirty." I knew what he meant. Moustached Alan was incredulous and patted me on the back. I took my umbrella and fake leather valise and sat in a coffee shop looking at employment ads. I had been studying hospitality at night and came across this one that said 'steward needed for silver service'. That's how I ended up at the Brisbane Club the same day I was sacked from AGC commercial leasing.

A few nights later, I was sitting at home in Spring Hill after a couple of beers tinkling with the piano when the phone rang. It was eight o'clock or so and someone yelled from upstairs that it was for me (no mobiles then). It was Alan.

"Hey Ste, what are you doing? Have you got the chess board set up and a couple of beers?"

I was surprised to hear his voice but he said he and ginger Alan would be there soon.

I pilfered some largies of Pilsener from Franco's fridge, sat them down opposite the chess board and began to pour glasses. I could tell they had already been on it for a while and when moustached Alan moved his first piece he said, "We both quit the same day you did." He didn't even flinch but looked calmly at me. Ginger Alan nodded affirmative to me as I sat holding my beer and thinking they were joking. They weren't. Ginger Alan moved his piece and they drank and then lifted their glasses to me draining the rest. Alan sort of vaguely apologised for getting me into that 'nest of shit' but I didn't blame him at all. Apparently, there was a rush for the door and seven or so had walked out that week. I don't think my Chinese mate Graham did though. Toupee Mike didn't last more than a month after that but the horror-faced secretary stayed on.

"Ste; we're setting up our own company on the Southside and we want you to be our office boy. Good pay, we'll look after you. You're alright." Ginger Alan nodded at me too while I filled their beers. The trust they were putting in me was enough to make me think that I must have done something right. I felt almost honoured that they would both walk away from their jobs as a result of my 'supposedly' unwarranted dismissal. They had obviously had this in the pipeline between them for a while and had discussed who would run the office. I was flattered. "How long have I got to think about it?"

"Now would be good Ste," he said again like David Caruso as he moved his next chess piece.

I explained that I had already found a job and maybe I'm not cut out for the (again) cut-throat world of finance. He threw the offer of an attractive weekly salary at me but I just couldn't see myself back in an office with a suit and tie hustling. He turned to me and nodded, finishing his beer and moved his last chess piece, checkmating ginger Alan saying, "See, I told you I was a better chess player than you." They rose, thanked me, shook my hand and left. I haven't seen either of them since. Thank you to both Alans; and the older Alan's advice about getting my hands dirty. I had been working at The Brisbane Club for three days and that was a much more enjoyable way to make money.

'There must be an easier way to make money.'

When I was a kid, my brother and I used to try and wangle money out of mum so we could buy lollies and play pinball at the corner shop across the road. Most of the time we did chores for nothing; mowing the lawn, cleaning the road grime off the windows, cleaning the bathroom etc. and of course we washed up, dried the dishes and put them away.

Once, mum said we could earn one cent per weed we pulled out of the lawn. We used bone-handled butter knives. It was mostly lambs tongue and dandelions but we agreed and said we would do it although at the time it seemed boring and time consuming. We started at the shaded side of the house and worked our way around to the front. After half an hour or so, my brother came up with the idea that we split each weed in half and double our income in half the time. When we counted out the weeds to get our one cent per weed we had over a hundred and forty but got busted on several split ones which we said had broken up when we threw them into the bucket.

Eventually, we got a dollar and spent the afternoon at the corner store clocking up replays on the pinball machine while eating an endless supply of bananas, musk sticks, raspberries and cobbers. Cobbers were one cent each, bananas; one cent for two; raspberries; five for a cent and musk sticks; two cents each. Game of pinball was twenty cents. Best spent dollar of my life.

'High finance.'

After my second year of grade twelve and having not received a T.E. (Tertiary Entrance) score that would enable me to study medicine or Physical Education teaching, I was given a reference from the friend of a family member (nepotism) who painted me in an employable light. This guy was a well-respected businessman, property valuer, something or other who owned more property than anyone else in the known universe at the time. (He knew the Main Roads Minister). Somehow I was led to an interview with a large Bank and was given a job as a batch clerk at the Lutwyche branch. Another Steve (who trained as an Olympic swimmer) mentored me for six months before I was transferred to Sandgate branch. It was a bit of a hike from Kedron at the time but in those days there was relatively no traffic on Sandgate road and I drove my recently purchased red and green Volkswagen Fastback to work in less than twenty minutes. The work was banal and repetitive. The early balding accountant, as they were called then, was a closed book and kept to himself and his own office. The secretary was a friendly, big-faced young woman of recent English immigration with a Farrah Fawcett haircut who helped me understand what was involved in the job. She and her husband owned an immaculate pair of regent green jags from the sixties. The first teller was a woman of about twenty three or so who I thought was rather aloof and self-assured. She had piercing blue eyes and a Hellenic nose but rarely engaged with me, looking through her straight blonde fringe occasionally to remind me of her status in the hierarchy. I couldn't guess what she looked like under the bank uniform and I had no idea she was eyeing me with a cougar's intent for belated and yearned-for procreation. She used a toothy professional smile when dealing with customers.

During this period I was experimenting with pot and on one occasion I got to work early, drove to the Sandgate beachside and smoked a joint. Surely no one would notice. After I had very quietly and discreetly done all my batch work, I settled in to read a novel I had started the night before. The English secretary, seeing my casual attitude to the job, chided me and said incredulously, "What are you doing?" I put the novel down and declared that I had finished my day's work and was waiting for something else to do. Before the boss arrived, she sent me out the back to the incinerator to burn old documents and cardboard boxes which had accumulated in the office. I thought, 'How good is this, burning stuff!' Needless to say, the boss did eventually call me into the office and said he was not impressed with my work ethic and if there was a family problem or personal issue, I should talk to him about it. To my utter amazement, he said, "I hope it's not something to do with drugs!" I assured him that it wasn't and I never again in my working life was 'under the influence' before work.

There were a few branch work parties at the Bracken Ridge Tavern on a Friday night where we would all turn up in our bank uniforms and proceed to eat and get pissed at the boss's expense. I was being kicked under the table by someone sitting across from me and kept moving my legs to avoid the contact lest they thought I was reciprocating. The English secretary eventually pulled me aside and told me that the aloof first teller was keen.

I had no idea. I always thought I was below her high status in the hierarchy. I returned to the table and looked directly into her very blue eyes thinking that I had never really looked at her before, thinking she was well out of my weight class. She smiled a toothy, sexy grin.

As it turned out, she drove me back to her place and we kissed and fondled each other into the early hours of Saturday morning. Being older and more experienced, she teased out the foreplay waiting for me to show how keen I was. It was several dates before we consummated the passion. We developed a relationship of sorts and the accountant found out somehow. He was miffed and she told me he had asked her out on a date which ended disastrously for her. "He's a pig," she said. I tried to think of what animal she would call me eventually but I only ever came up with 'randy ram' or 'cougars lunch.' She liked me for some reason and I didn't resist the onslaught. One night in that little fibro half-house in Sandgate, a massive storm swept through while we were in bed and smashed all the walls, windows and roof until there was almost nothing left. It was terrifying to say the least. Luckily, she was renting at the time. We tip-toed through the glass with our meagre possessions and found an alternative abode.

I would drive from Kedron to Sandgate to spend nights with her until late and then drive home to Kedron only to drive back to Sandgate the next morning for work. Sometimes I got clever and took my work clothes with me to stay the night.

I was earning close to three hundred dollars a week which was enough to pay my board at home, petrol for my car (19 cents a litre) and the occasional dinner. Sometimes I would go shopping for work clothes or 'going out' gear which in 1979 included lots of maroon flares , matching platform shoes and a white and maroon body shirt for dancing . Things seemed to be going swimmingly in Sandgate as my new girlfriend met my friends and we sort of partied and fell into a deep relationship. She was more than four years older than me but we seemed to click better than any of the relationships I'd had with girls who were supposed to be traditionally two years younger than me. Then the unexpected transfer to Toowoomba appeared on my desk. Yes, I was to work in Ruthven Street Toowoomba while my girlfriend was to remain at Sandgate. Somehow, I thought it was all a ploy by the accountant to get rid of me so he could have another attempt at wooing her but she assured me that he was a cold fish and she was not interested. I found a cheap boarding house in Rangeville and moved in with my clothes and my XY wagon.

The Ruthven Street branch at Toowoomba was quite a big bank catering for town locals and farmers from further afield. I met an elderly customer who was quite wealthy called Alga Slime (true!) She would come into the bank merely to check her massive balance.

The balding, bespectacled accountant, Jim, would often warn me from a distance not to enter his glass enclosed office as I approached by saying that he'd been 'farting like a horse all morning'. I worked with a woman called Catherine, an officious batch clerk who took me to the drive-in one night and offered to fellate me in preference to penetrative sex. She wore panty hose as a defence mechanism. I don't remember the film.

Jane was a tall, good looking girl from Mitchell with an honest smile whose family owned a large property. She was friendly and hardworking, helping me to do the job I wasn't sure of. (I recently saw her, 2016, with her husband and children at the Point Cartwright Water tower and recognised her immediately despite the span of thirty years.) She was a lovely girl. Hi Jane.

Then there was Ron, who was the total anathema to what anyone would think was a typical bank employee. Ron had a snow man type figure with long oily hair, thick lensed glasses portraying beady eyes, a half-hearted attempt at an Amish beard, which was really just lazy shaving, and a voice that would peel paint from the space shuttle. He would appear back at his desk at lunchtime and suck the meat out of a pie as though it was the end of a milkshake through a straw. Whether he was happy or angry, his faced appeared to be sucking in towards his nose in a snarl of confusion. His mouth moved like Clutch Cargo.

Satisfied with his noisy consumption, he would also gulp down a coke to help with his digestion. He was the original nerd who used to talk about Dungeons and Dragons and anything to do with the latest technology of the time. The girls would give him a wide berth (which he was painfully aware of) but I gave him the time to talk to me while he leaned his gut over my desk saying that he had finished all his work and advised me on how to do the same thing. He lived with his mum and told me in no uncertain terms that they couldn't sack him because he was too good at this job and they couldn't do without him because of his knowledge of computers at the time (1979 DOS). He probably went on to make millions.

My job was to trammel through the cheques and make sure the signatures matched. How would I know? I recognised a few big clients' signatures but then had to verify anything that looked suspicious by going to the client's file and checking the original monikers. There were lunchtime drinks on occasions at the White Horse Hotel across the road leaving me drunkenly faking the rest of the afternoon going through accounts pretending I was ensconced in my work while I was secretly looking at Jane or writing poems.

At this time I was boarding with a family in Rangeville who had three sons, triplets, who were in the Army, Navy, and Air Force. I never met any of them. There were also two daughters who were in the Army and Air Force and the youngest girl named Bubby who was still at school, in the Girl Guides but aspired to be in the Armed Forces like her parents, brothers and sisters. Only Bubby lived at home then as all the others lived on base. Their mother was ex-army and a strange bod indeed, while her husband, who was ex-Air Force, now worked at the Air Force warehouse in Dalby. He would come home and sit in the lounge room pretending to read the paper but falling asleep while his strange wife would cook sausages and frozen potato gems for dinner. It was here that I found the guitar which I tuned to their out-of-tune piano and began to teach myself to alleviate my boredom.

Someone at work asked me to join the squash club for a Wednesday B Grade competition and I found myself enjoying a healthy physical outlet which kept me away from the strangely, passive militant, family I was boarding with. I began to frequent the gym and heated pool looking for an outlet to my pent up frustrations as a bank Johnny. After a swim and a workout, I met a jockey wearing a wetsuit in the sauna who was trying to lose 6kilos before the race tomorrow. He hadn't eaten for twenty hours and wouldn't til after the race.

I drove to Sandgate each weekend to see my girlfriend while listening to cassette tapes of Pink Floyd's 'The Wall' or Chick Corea's 'My Spanish Heart' because they both lasted ninety minutes which was the time it took me to drive my Ford XY station wagon from Toowoomba to Sandgate. My new Clarion stereo made the trip so much more pleasant.

One of the older girls in the military family (none of whom had seen any action) asked me to take her to the Air Force Ball. I think her mother had suggested it and I flippantly agreed to accompany her to the ball. I shouldn't have. I was inconsiderate and I now apologise, 32 years later.

As the date of the ball drew nearer and they hadn't reminded me that it was 'this' weekend I had to admit that I had an important date with my girlfriend and couldn't attend. There were groans of disbelief as I departed Friday night on my weekly pilgrimage to Sandgate. I felt some pangs of guilt as I drove well over the speed limit to get to my destination while Chick Corea played 'Love Castle'. The boarding family all knew I had a girlfriend but somehow they also believed that I was going to forego my relationship to accompany their 22 year-old daughter to a ball where I may have been a possible addition to their unmarried daughter's scant years of serious relationships. I was meant to be an unexpected coup in her otherwise sparsely populated attempts to attract a suitable partner who would be content to breed more of the same unspectacular military dross who were not presently at war. But that's just my subjective version of what I thought they were thinking. (Sorry), I'd had a similar experience with a staff member of KFC when I was sixteen. (Another story perhaps?)

When I returned to the boarding house early on Monday morning, I was greeted with indifference and silence. Needless to say, I left the bank in Toowoomba not long after, having secured a transfer to Leichardt Street in Fortitude Valley in Brisbane. Thus ended my country service; my relationship with my girlfriend and any connection with the military family of Toowoomba. I had earned enough money to buy petrol, clothes, beer and accumulate some savings while I was in that lovely country town and met some wonderful people who changed my view of the world. It's also where I taught myself to play guitar.

Once I was back in the big smoke, I really didn't fit. I looked at my overweight, balding accountant to my left and my even more overweight boss in his office to my right under the fluoro lights and realized I didn't want to be that person having long unhealthy lunches, chasing money and counting other people's coins. I wanted to be outside in the sunshine running wild and not answerable to anyone. I was earning well over $350 per week by now but it was not what I imagined to be a fulfilling career. I was living with my school mate Gavin while he was at Uni studying physics and pure maths. We played Bowie and Stones records at night occasionally imbibing in leafy comestibles. We had dress-up parties where we were all playing guitars or singing. It was a fun time but I still found time to write soppy poems late at night.

During this time at the Leichardt Street bank I met an artist from Hawaii. We got on famously even though she was eight years my senior. I got busted for possession while living with my old school friend and I escaped to Marcus Beach looking for solitude with my newly found American friend, Lily Bell. She was a talented artist and a lovely person who encouraged me to play music and write. I didn't need any encouragement to write because I had been writing since I was quite young; poems, songs and stories. I applied for the dole but had to wait six weeks to get paid. By the time I got any money I'd already found work.

'Bohemian lifestyle.'

That was where I began catching sand worms during the days and working for the Marcus Xavier catering company at Luther Heights in the early mornings and evenings. Life was good, although a bit hand to mouth on occasions trying to make the rent, but generally I was not working in the bank and I could go outside to the beach anytime I felt the urge. We met some strange characters through the next door neighbour in our townhouse. Annie, in number 2, was a qualified nurse (apparently) but wore rose coloured glasses and psychedelic clothes that smelled of frankincense and fennel tea. She was proud to be an Aries and occasionally offered me massages for no particular remedial reason.

She had all types of herbs and chicory coffee and lemongrass in her kitchen with a variety of healing teas which I wasn't sure were exactly what she said they were. The fenugreek tea stunk like cats piss coming out of her skin. She was very forthright and would demand I lay down on the mattress under the stairwell so she could give me a relaxing massage. I took off my shirt but she insisted I had to be naked. I resisted the request and left my scoops on. She plied me with some extremely sweet-smelling oil which assaulted my olfactory senses and emphasised the pain of the, quite frankly, very ordinary massage. She could tell I was tense and tried to force me to relax with harsh probing thumbs. I gave in a little hoping she would tire and give up so I could escape the sickly sweet smell. As she finished, I went to get up and she said, "No! Just lie there for a minute. There's no hurry."

I stayed for a polite and tortured couple of minutes trying to breathe through my mouth.

She used to make these cotton fisherman's pants in bright colours and stripes. She gave me a pair of dark blue with rainbow stripes down the leg and when all my friends saw them, bought their own from Annie for fifteen dollars a pop. Needless to say, I got kickbacks from these sales in the form of herbs, accoutrement and friendly massages.

Annie's friend 'Noddy' used to visit from his property at Mapleton to stay with her. He was an artist who painted cockatoos and parrots on to Annie's homemade cotton jackets and the occasional denim jacket. They were beautiful and very unique. Noddy also owned a property down the forestry road. He grew exotic fruits like longans and exported them overseas. In the growing season he would hire WOOFAS and then during the harvest season, would go to Pakistan to watch the cricket with his hippy friends from the seventies.

They would share photographs of their visits to Nepal while drinking Guinness at the Mapleton Hotel. Years later, I was privy to one of these occasions during my lunchtime at the Mapleton School and was fascinated by the candid photos from another world.

I earnt money from the catering company, catching worms, playing music with a vertically challenged friend of Annie's, Billy Flynn (who sorta played piano, drove a giant convertible Cadillac and ironically, was a window cleaner part time). I was promoting Lily's art and selling 'interesting comestibles' through my contacts in the mountains and Noosa. I could afford to pay rent and petrol and still go out and eat at good restaurants. I knew people who would vouch for me in any and all situations. It was a very artistic community and I seemed to fit right in even though I had nothing artistic to contribute. I wrote songs and poems when the moment took me and surfed a lot. Embarrassingly, I still have some of those hand-written pieces on faded yellow paper. We then moved from Marcus Beach to Noosa. Lily's friend Alice came to live with us for a while and we were a happy artistic threesome.

Occasionally, Lily and I would go to the Cloudland markets in Brisbane and she would draw caricatures of people in profile for three bucks a pop. She displayed the drawing on an overhead projector which everyone could see emerging on the screen. She drew deftly left- handed and rarely had to start again. People would gladly pay me three dollars to have a framed cartoon image to take with them; A genuine 'Lily Bell' original. It took her about a minute or so to finish each piece and when there was a line up, she would do six or seven in a row before resting her fingers. Hundreds of people would flock to those markets buying whatever the latest 'craze' was at the time. Clothes, plants, nick nacks, crystals and of course, a portrait of yourself in cartoon style. Some days we took home three hundred dollars. That was good tax free money in 1980 when our three-storey Spanish style unit was $85 per week. We drove back to Noosa in our faded grey 1962 VW beetle singing Beatles songs.

I played with 'Nurse' Annie's short-arsed friend Billy in a couple of venues in Noosa and busked in Hastings Street a few times. Usually in an evening, we would make between 50 and

100 dollars each, including a drink and food rider. When I was relaxing at night, with my usual relaxants, I would write corny poems and sentimental songs. Blur this scene into wavy lines.

'Respect your elders.'

In another time and place, far removed from my seaside sojourn, I found myself as the manager of the Redcliffe Bowls Club. I decided to maintain my standards, according to my hospitality mentor Tom, choosing to wear the bowtie and black and whites all the time. I ran the bar and had the cleaning contract. With my experience at the Brisbane Club I could easily manage the day to day running of the bar and serve the members quickly between 'ends'. The current drunken provedore, jealous of my new position in the club, made his opinion of me very clear. "Who do you think you are, Superman?" he would say in a drunken slur. "What's with the fucking bow-tie Steve? You can take that off!" I never did.

Spearing kegs and cleaning the beer lines every night (only three kegs of XXXX, Gold and some Carlton beer) was not that difficult. I would clean the toilets, mop out the bar, vacuum the main areas and go home with a six pack or a bottle of complimentary Bundy rum every few days. I'd been in worse financial situations.

Every Saturday, the treasurer would arrive before opening and do the tills checking to see that all the money was in the safe. Sometimes he would tell me that the money in the safe was more than was on the till and hand me a fifty dollar bill as a weekly tip. With my generous wage and cleaning fee, I was earning $550 dollars per week, plus free take home alcohol of my choice (up to a point) and the occasional bonus for a good week's earnings. I was also given sandwiches from the women players on

Tuesdays and, on mixed Wednesdays, when everyone brought a plate; I would be invited to partake of triangle sandwiches, of varied fillings, for lunch. A good life, genuine people and to my surprise, stories I had never heard before from men and women of a bygone era.

Where do I begin with such a rich vein of nearly forgotten history so that I don't leave anyone out and don't exclude the details? I can't, of course, recall all those stories, but I can mention some of the characters who made my job more satisfying than anything I had ever done before. These were people who had shaped the life I live now and who had survived the inexcusable atrocities of war. They all gathered to play bowls with a determined sense of life, fun and companionship. I felt privileged to be serving these venerable elders who were enjoying their twilight years as though they were naughty teenagers. And they were naughty in ways that I had never imagined elderly people to be. Widowers and widows flirted; men drank, swore, bowled and told tall tales while the white-uniformed women gaggled excitedly sipping weak brandy lime and soda and shandies. The ladies told me they thought my bow-tie had lifted the standard in the club. I thanked them and served each patron with a professional smile as I had been taught by my elderly mentor Tom. It worked. My efforts to give good service had been noticed and appreciated. I was serving alcohol to the elderly. Yay! I also learned to bowl and accompanied some of the members to drunken competitions at Deception Bay or Bramble Bay. How did we get home after two or five pots and 12 ponies?

They told stories that I never doubted were true, while they sipped their small drinks. There was rarely more than a few minutes of conversation at a time between ends. When they came for the next drink I would ask them to continue the story. They would know exactly where they had left off and proceeded to tell the rest of the story with not a shred of mental debilitation evident, despite the obvious continual consumption of alcohol. Everyone wanted to tell me something of their past and I was like a conduit absorbing each face and emotion as I poured their favourite imbibement. Welsh Guard, Rats of Tobruk, G Force and all the ranks and dogs tags in between. Their lust for life was inspiring to say the least and I was only 24.

During quiet moments, I would write a story about one of them. I had a blotting pad of blank pages called 'Things to Do' printed by the local newspaper, 'The Redcliffe Herald'. I wrote the outline for a story on eight pages before I got to 'part two' (which I extended some years later to twenty three pages). I have paraphrased that story to save you from the exhaustion of reading the whole thing although I'm sure it will be available on my extensive catalogue available in 2023. This story is about Taffy. I never knew his real name, although 'Selwyn' pops into my head as I write this. He was just known as Taffy to everyone.

"Call me Taffy laddie," he said excitedly extending his hand in introduction and shook it firmly.

"Nice to meet you Taffy, I'm Steve." I looked directly into his pale blue eyes and they smiled. I could tell he was still vibrant and had lived a good life. He groomed himself well and was physically quite mobile for an eighty four year old. He only bowled socially, not competitively.

"Give us a black and tan Steve," he said scoping the room. He corrected my amounts of stout and beer to suit his purposes. "That's it." He nodded and sipped the drink until his Don Amice moustache was hidden under the brown foam. I indicated to his lip and he licked it and then wiped it with the back of his hand and looked at me to see if he had cleared it. I nodded.

"Steve, if I was young and good looking like you, I'd be down the Gold Coast trying to get some of them old rich bitches." He smiled cheekily and sipped his brew.

"See that one over there?" He looked over his shoulder but I could only see three women sitting at a table all dressed in white bowls uniforms. They all looked the same to me.

"The one in the middle, she could be my third wife." His eyebrows raised high at me and I tried to determine the features of the woman he had indicated. I felt like I was an eight year old child trying to guess the atomic weight of magnesium. They wore the same hair styles under their hats and looked as generic as any of the other women in that establishment except this woman was looking in the direction of the bar where Taffy and I were trying to pretend that we weren't talking about them; but we were.

He was randy and ready. He walked over to the table and sat down with them pointing to the bar. They waved at me and I smiled back. The two other women left and Taffy was alone with his girlfriend who may become wife number three. He was eighty four and she was seventy five.

Later that afternoon, after a dozen or so 'ponies' (5oz beers), Taffy kissed his girlfriend on the cheek goodbye and rallied back to the bar for last drinks. He was a bit drunk, but so were others who came for their 'last nips'. I sold more in the last hour before closing than throughout the whole day. "Giss a nip 'o' whiskey Stevie," The Scottish Rats of Tobruk would relay stories of their ventures in Egypt, George would tell of an incursion with Z Force and the Welsh guard would share his stories about protecting the young Queen Elizabeth who would step outside her balcony to make the guards stand to attention and then duck inside again and back out as soon as they relaxed. "Bloody little mischievous one that," he would say scoffing his last whiskey. Everyone would laugh and try to order another even though it was past closing at six o'clock. I poured everyone their last drinks hoping to extend the stories but said, "If anyone comes in here now, I poured these before closing time OK?" They would roar with laughter and then whack their paper cash on the bar to secure another 'wee dram'. Taffy was always last to leave. He would hang around while I was cleaning and talk of his previous wives while helping himself to another whiskey. Sometimes he would try to help by pushing in chairs and collecting glasses. I could tell he was lonely and that he was prolonging that moment when he would go home and have to deal with his own company as he had done for many years. I was perhaps what he had been when he was my age in 1924. As I locked the front door of the club one night, he turned to me and invited me to his house for a night cap. His house adjoined the bowls club fence through a gate so I accepted. It was only seven o'clock and I needed a break from the semi-frantic day.

Once inside his humble house, I saw a different Taffy. He relaxed and his posture slumped a little but he was the consummate host producing delicate crystal beer glasses and pouring us a good foam from a largey of Pilsener he kept stocked in his fridge. He showed me his house and furniture including a large red and green Genoa lounge. When we sat down to talk he seemed to go back sixty years and relate stories of himself dressed in white suits surrounded by beautiful women on a cruise ship. He showed me a photo of exactly that moment but as he went on he seemed overtaken by a sadness that he could not shed from his memory and began to relate the first love of his life. I sipped the beer and patiently listened. I imagined him as the dashing young twenty-four year old in the photograph. But there was regret too. His first wife had died (he didn't say how) and he remarried two years later. She also went off to war as a nurse but he didn't see her again.

His hair became wispy and grey in the poor light of the 40 watt bulb and he looked at the floor remembering. I finished my beer and rose to leave. It wasn't the last time I had a knock off drink with Taffy but he had made an indelible mark on my psyche, making me think that one day, I might be like him. I eventually bought his red and green Genoa lounge in mint condition (no dust! he demonstrated by slapping each of the fat cushions) and dragged it around for another twenty years. He gave me some crystal glasses and a beer bottle opener which he had bought in 1953 from some exotic location. I still have them.

The bowls club was the hub of social activity for the over 50's although some younger members were beginning to frequent the club as the sport became international.

Bertie was a very thin man of about 90 who walked with little shuffling steps. He had a quiet wispy voice and had apparently served in one of the Special Forces. He shuffled into the toilet and this huge man, Dennis, who was 6'6" and built like a giant, left the bar and followed Bertie in and stood next to him at the urinal. Bertie shuffled out minutes later followed by Dennis who returned to the bar shaking his head side to side.

"Cheesus," Dennis said rolling his eyes. "Bertie's hung like a fuckin dinosaur. If he'd have hiccupped, he would have drained the urinal." I snorted a laugh as did the others sitting within earshot and we all turned to watch Bertie carefully negotiating the stairs back to the bowling green. Go Bertie!

"Yep, he's popular with the ladies; that's for sure," said another drinker and we laughed again.

Dennis Plant was of English origin and I asked him flippantly if he was related to Robert. "Yeh, he's my cousin." I quickly guessed his age and thought he could have been telling the truth. The following Saturday he brought in a Led Zeppelin album signed by Robert Plant 'to Dennis.' Initially he wanted to give it to me but his wife heard of my enthusiasm and he had to keep it. "It could be worth something Dennis," she said. He also told me that he used to play the lotto regularly with the same numbers. The week his numbers came up on the TV screen he leaped for joy in the lounge room thrusting his hand into the overhead fan, only to realise his ticket was sitting on the fridge and he'd neglected to lodge it that week. He sported a plaster cast on his fingers for six weeks and drank a lot of beer.

That particular Saturday was club championship day and one of the busiest in the Club's calendar. The beer was flowing from early morning. Little Mick had bought in the ice, Big Bill the sand crabs and extra kegs were delivered by the XXXX rep. Mick and Bill got a complimentary three pots for their services and it wasn't even 9 0'clock. Oops!

The ponies and pots lined the bar during the fiercely fought competition on the green. Some were there to defend their title but most were there as a social event. Men and women competed on their own greens and while most of the women drank tea in the dining room, most of the men made use of their downtime in the doubles to line up drinks for their mates. I was busy and occasionally got a hand from the president who would step in and pour pots. His wife Dorothy (assisted by Ida and Ivy) would be directing traffic in the dining room as she was the women's president. By lunchtime most of the bowlers had migrated into the dining room for some sandwiches and saveloys or sausage rolls. The bar quietened down a bit and a man to my left asked for a refill. I'd seen him on Saturdays every now and then. He introduced himself with a slurred speech but I knew he was not drunk. "I'm Mike". He was a member of the club but not a bowler.

Mike told me he had had an accident which left his brain a bit damaged and affected his speech and memory. He was 43 and used to work at the airport but now had a good job at Luggage Point. Earlier in the day, when the president was checking the calendar for another event, Mike overheard him and correctly said that the day he'd chosen was a Saturday and wouldn't be suitable for a mixed competition. The president did not take much notice and looked at his diary for another day. Mike, again, told him it was a Tuesday within seconds.

When there was a lull in the beer traffic, I returned to Mike with a wall calendar which I placed on the counter under the bar where he couldn't see it.

"How did you do that Mike? That's amazing." He smiled and told me that after his accident, his uncle showed him this trick to help with his memory. It was the 5th March and I flipped down the calendar to August.

"What's the 8th August?" He did a quick calculation in his head and told me it was a Sunday.

"How far forward can I go?" I asked.

"Yeh, just tell me the year and I'll adjust the key day to work it out." I was flabbergasted and curious to learn how he did it. The bar started to get busy as the bowlers charged up before the next round and I became distracted. Half an hour and a keg change later, I went back to Mike to ask him to explain but he drained his beer and left saying, "I can only have three Steve and then I have to go. See you next Saturday." I thanked him and waved as I pondered his strange secret.

"Giss a black 'n' tan Stevie," said Taffy, already well on the way.

"And two ponies and a dram, thanks Stevie," yelled the Scottish Rats.

"And two pots for myself and my partner Bertie," Z Force George asked politely looking very much like Burt Lancaster. Bertie stood quietly, smiling, alongside George looking like his shadow. Re-charged, they left for the final few ends of the competition.

As the games ended they poured into the bar. Everyone was on a high as they tried to present the results next door amongst the din of the bar. For a while, everyone politely shut up while the champions were presented their trophies and applauded. Many of the women disappeared quickly but the bar was licensed on this day to open til 7 so it was noisy for another hour and a half. The president again stepped in to help me but poured his and his mates drinks first and then drank it from behind the bar. Taffy and the Welsh guard started to sing an old WW2 era song (insert appropriate song here, Tipperary?) and to my surprise everyone joined in with full voice and commitment. They could all sing in key and with amazing volume. Even the ones who couldn't sing would sing with gusto.

I stood listening and watching the emotion on their faces and my eyes welled up. I joined with snippets of the songs that I knew but would not have been heard in that room if I'd yelled fire at the top of my voice. For a while, someone played the piano next door and started up another round of belting songs. It was obvious to me that these men had shared something deeper than any generation alive. They were singing the song of victory and survival and lamenting lost mates and celebrating their families and each other.

Though they came from different parts of the world, England, Scotland, Wales, Ireland, Germany, Lebanon, France, America,

Italy, they were tied together in a moment which forged friendships that were closer than any sports team or tribe could hope for. They were the 'post-war' family and despite their petty arguments they loved and respected each other. They danced and sang and played and drank and all looked forward to the next occasion where they could celebrate being alive and watch their grandchildren grow up. I was lucky to be there managing the club when it was in its heyday. I felt there was a reason that I was there at that time. Call it fate or whatever, I watched and listened and recorded as much as I could in my memory and by writing some down. Somehow, I have perpetuated their lives through my memory and now they live on, playing, singing and dancing.

A couple of Saturdays later Mike arrived and I was determined to ask him again about his ability to tell what day any given date was on the calendar. I served him a pot when in walked the goop-goop brothers. These two were mates who drove a removalist truck. They were both big men and I knew they were on a lunch break. I poured their schooners quickly knowing they were on a time limit. They both picked up the schooners and gulped them down in one go. I had already begun to pour their second, knowing they would have a third and possibly a fourth, besides, it was cheap to drink at the Bowls Club if you were a member. The second schooner went down as quickly as the first, goop, goop, goop; hence the nickname I had given them, the 'goop-goop brothers'. Mike was watching from the side of the bar as they slowed down on the third round. I had just enough time to refill Mike before the next two schooners were ordered. They sat on these for about five minutes in all, thanked me on the way out and got into their truck to do the next two removals for the afternoon. The legal limit for driving under the influence was still 0.08 then but I'm not sure what their reading would have been if they'd been pulled over. Apparently, they would also visit other clubs during the day so it was hard to tell how much they had consumed on any given Saturday. I served a few more bowlers and kept my eye on Mike to make sure he hadn't finished his second beer. I walked over to him and asked about the date thing.

"It's a bit complex Steve and you have to remember twelve numbers which you use for each month. Give us a bit of paper." My blotting pad was there in a second and he began to draw up a chart with all the months of the year and beside each month was written a number. I was distracted by a member and went to serve him a couple of ponies.

When I returned to Mike, he asked for his third beer and then showed me the list of months. "It's easier to remember the numbers if you split them into 3 lots of 4," he said looking at me with steel blue eyes and lisping out of the left side of his mouth.

J-2
F-5
M-5
A-1
••••••
M-3
J-6
J-1
A-4
••••••

S-0
O-2
N-5
D-0

"If the date is Jan 14th you add the 2 for January making it sixteen then divide by 7.

14+2=16   16/7=2 remainder 2. The remainder is the important bit.

"There is a key day for each year, let's say in this case, 1984, it's Monday. You count two from Monday; Tuesday, Wednesday and you realise that the 14th Jan is a Wednesday. Now you try it." He handed me the paper but again I had to serve the bar. I was distracted for long enough that Mike had finished his third beer and was walking out waving at me.

"Wait up a minute Mike," I called over the noisy crowd. He turned and looked at me and lingered near the end of the bar long enough for me to ask him what the key day was for this year and how do I find the next one. People were queuing at the bar impatiently.

"This year is Monday, next year, Tuesday and so on until you reach a leap year and change the key day on the 29th February." He waved and I nodded, still not sure if I understood completely. By the time I had closed up at five o'clock I had been thinking about the formula for three hours. I picked up the list and a calendar and tried it for myself. On the third go I hit the jackpot and began memorising the numbers for each month as I cleaned the bar and whistled some old tune the Scotsmen had been singing. 2551, 3614, 0250 over and over again. Once home, I wrote my own version and tested it out on my girlfriend who had her work diary in front of her. She was suitably impressed but couldn't work out why this skill would be important for anything other than guessing the day of a certain date. Fair enough.

Over the years I have showed countless numbers of people (who may have been interested) including students and friends but a lot of people forgot the key numbers for each month unless they had written them down. I'm proud to say that I have remembered them.

As I write this, it is the 27th May 2020, add 3 makes 30, divide by 7=4 remainder 2. The key day for 2020 is Monday; add 2 and today is Wednesday. Don't count the key day! This became a valuable memory exercise when I began my tertiary education. I had applied to study, left the club and didn't have the opportunity to thank Mike as I never saw him again. Thanks Mike. He would be 79 now and his birthday was on the 23/6 which was a Tuesday.

At the end of 2019 my wife and I were in Redcliffe shopping for a campervan. After looking at the arcade dedicated to the 'Bee Gees', she wandered off to scour the op shops and I walked around the corner to where the bowls club used to be. It was no longer a bowls club. The greens were vast, weedy, unkempt lawns bordered by thirty year old palm trees. Inside the building to the left was a door opening into a billiards club and to the right, through another door, a women's group with tables full of craft and knitting etc. There was no sign of the old club. I spoke to no-one and walked out towards the greens looking from the top step at what had been a vibrant social and sporting venue. I realised that *virtually* none of those people would be alive today and yet somehow I have perpetuated their stories into the future. With a deep sigh and fond memories I walked down the path and glanced over at Taffy's old house. It was now a renovated two story unit complex filling up the entire block. I wondered for a minute if the ghost of Taffy had been seen singing in the hallways of the building late at night.

I felt some closure at that moment, knowing that the job I did there had given me a renewed respect for all those men and women who served our country, ensuring that we and future generations of Australians, live in a free democratic society. Thank you.

And thanks for the bonuses Mr Treasurer. I'd managed to save some money for the next stage of my life; whatever that may be. This was 1984 and we had all read George Orwell and were still listening to David Bowie's song of the same name but where was Big Brother my friends? Little did we know, he was lurking just around the corner.

'Sometimes you've just gotta do what you've gotta do...'

Some years before this, I had returned to Brisbane after my Marcus Beach sea-change, worm-catching jaunt and managed to finagle a job at a large auto parts company in Turbot St. It was a massive, poorly lit and aged office space. There were glass-petitioned offices for the managers and everyone else was plonked haphazardly wherever there was a desk near a phone line. The interview, which I realised later, included the same three questions I was asked at the finance company jobs. I started that friday, not knowing what I was really supposed to be doing and then Nigel taught me everything I needed to know about the job after the half hour lunch break which lasted til one o'clock. Thanks Nige.

On Monday, I turned up at work with plaster on my right arm from wrist to shoulder. My new boss looked at me with disbelief and I explained it was a 'grass skiing' accident. He shrugged and looked at me incredulously. This was the last thing he needed on a Monday.

"What are you gonna do? You can't write anything or use the phone proplly."

I'd thought about it the night before and replied, demonstrating my newly acquired skill of writing with my left hand.

"I'll write in red and I can use one of those shoulder-phone-holder things," that was all the rage at the time for any serious businessman as ear phones are today.

He paused, thinking about my proposition and then waved me back to my desk.

"We'll see how you go," he said rather patiently for a boss who had just hired a crippled clerk. I managed to work in that condition for five weeks perfecting my left-handedness and juggling the phone on my shoulder. As part of the job I had spoken to people working at the 'warehouse' in Hendra including my colleague, Nigel, who'd trained me for half an hour, and who had recently been hired as assistant office manager at the warehouse.

"It's great Steve, you'd fit right in. There's a job going here and it's better than working for that prick in town. Let me know and I'll set up an interview with our boss."

I thought about it on the way home and through the night. I was due to get my plaster off and I was living closer to the 'warehouse' than the city. It was a very unexciting job in Turbot St. and I felt like a number earning minimum wage filling in time. I had no urge to go up the ranks of management, yawn! I wanted to get my hands dirty.

The next day was belting rain as I walked from the large dirt carpark in James St. to work. I was carrying my usual valise/ briefcase (containing nothing important) in my left hand and trying as best I could to keep the umbrella over my head with my plastered arm. My fake leather shoes were soaked and the rain came in sideways wetting my plaster and shirt. Then, I saw them; sheltering under a small half-demolished archway, laughing as though they didn't have a care in the world. Soaked and drunk and homeless, they seemed happy like Ren and Stimpy. Well, one of them seemed happy and the other one was quietly sipping his deathly brew and nodding like a puppy in agreeance while chuckling mischievously.

They were wearing cheap suits of dubious age, size and condition and both brandished a bottle of what I could only assume was cheap brandy or Metho in a paper bag. As I approached them in my sodden work garb they were half way through some alcohol-induced metaphysical conversation, raving, laughing. The rain was pelting so hard it was coming back up from the ground but they were crouched in this little circular recess unaffected by the rest of the world or the weather. I stopped and turned to face them listening to the mindless raving. Eventually, they looked at me with blank, bewildered faces like two school boys who've been caught smoking at the bus stop with their uniforms on.

"What are you doing?" I yelled over the rain, incredulous to see two grown men flagrantly wasting their lives. "Why don't you go and get a job?" It was ten to eight in the morning. The one with the fogged up milk-bottle glasses mumbled something I didn't hear. The other just sighed, "Yeah, ya got a smoke?" I walked off. They returned to their conversation as though I was a wraith that had appeared to them from a nightmare and then melted into the grey veil of rain.

Frustratedly drenched and cold, I walked on towards the office shaking my head with drips of rain flying from my nose and hair. In that moment, I pictured myself with one of my friends, having lost everything, doing the same thing. I wondered what could drive a person to that level of 'not giving a shit'. Did I give a shit, standing sopping wet in my new boring job?

I made up my mind in the short time it took me to compose my 'soaked' self and sit at my desk, that I would never be either of those people. I would take the job at the warehouse and find something new. I needed to move on. The thought of those two men haunted me for a long time afterwards. I told people what I had seen that day and there was always a moment of disbelief in their face but maybe I felt it wasn't a story I was supposed to tell others, but rather, a moment just for me; to highlight the options of life, to remind me of the possibilities of our choices and that everyone can choose their own destiny; or not? I wrote some sad stories and poems (left-handed) in my down-time at that job.

I felt no guilt about writing down my feelings into rhyme or songs while I was pretending to work and being paid shit wages. Honestly, the décor and lighting were depressing enough to make anyone reconsider their life choices and jump out the window of the ground floor office. It just so happened, that it was me who wanted to flee.

"I want to go and work at the warehouse," I said blandly to my boss, still dripping onto his nylon-carpeted office floor. He looked at my bedraggled figure and raised his shoulders and hands.

"Why? It's a shit hole down there. You'll never get ahead in that place." He looked like he had more on his mind than my dilemma and agreed to phone the manager of the warehouse and hook me up with the available job. He told me quietly his wife was not well and that he also was leaving his job to look after her. I didn't know what to say.

I always found him to be a reasonably approachable and understanding fortyish man trying to find his way in the universe as we all were; including the two drunk bums sitting in the alcove in the rain that morning, in a semi-demolished building, laughing. I felt somewhere in between those two extremes; or was I envious of the bums? Or was it the Rosicrucian monographs I was reading at night? Or was it just me?

That was the end of my $275.50 per week job at Turbot Street in the Valley. We were still paid with little paper pay packets full of cash, counted out by the efficient office girls, after being delivered by the 'Brinks' armoured truck every Friday. Everyone tried to think of the perfect heist when the truck full of money turned up but it was all wishful thinking, like winning the Lotto. Lorenzo, from collections, knew I had worked at the bank and asked me to check his pay every week counting out the paper bills while licking my fingers. I'd slam them on the desk in front of him counting aloud so he could check he was being paid the amount he was promised like a true Roman. There were no tearful goodbyes from that job.

'God helps those who help themselves.'

On Monday I started at the warehouse trying to dispel thoughts of those two professional bums sitting in the rain, at eight in the morning, drinking and laughing their lives away until ... what? An ambulance picked them up in the park, in winter, lonely, starving and wracked with pneumonia and lice? 'At least I have a job' I thought and this was to be 'one' of more than 'forty!'

The picking room at the warehouse was great. A line of ten or so guys of differing builds and ages, sitting on stools facing a common wall of notes and parts numbers, answering the phone to mechanics, engineers, businesses and anything to do with automotive parts who may have needed a '3417' for an RX4. The three huge six-inch-thick volumes of car parts was available to everyone but sometimes you had to steal someone else's while you were on the phone and they were all tethered to the wall to prevent theft. Why, I don't know.

It was difficult to hear the person on the phone as all ten spoke at once trying to get their message through and finish the order so they could hang up and get another call. There were bonuses for volume and number of calls. The more efficient you were, the more you were appreciated. German efficiency? I learned the lingo quickly and asked if I wasn't sure. After taking the phone order, I would go out into the warehouse, find the parts that had been ordered and place them in a large 'Bunning's style' trolley. Sometimes we would do two or three orders in a row to save time. Dave showed me how to minimize my time in the racks so we could duck out for a smoke and not be missed.

Dave was animated with a good sense of humour and a self-deprecating manner that no-one would challenge, mainly because he was only 4' 8 1/2" tall. He whistled and laughed as he went about his job, happy with his marriage and three children. He told me about his three year old walking in on him and his wife having sex one morning and asking, "Why are you trying to kill mummy?" "I'm not killing mummy, I'm taking her to heaven."

We would deliver the parts to the packaging section with a copy of the order where the two butch lesbians would box them up and get the driver to deliver them all over north Brisbane. I moved around a bit from taking orders, picking parts, serving the front counter and eventually ended up as a delivery driver (and part-time packer when one of the girls didn't come in.) The boss wanted me to move into the office but I was content with the relative freedom of driving all over North Brisbane delivering spare parts. There was no two-way radio or mobile phone to answer to and often my deliveries allowed me a bit of down time where I would go and have lunch or go home for a coffee and smoke and watch afternoon TV. When asked about the delay I would say there was an accident or heavy traffic.

On occasions I was able to slip a few tools and parts for friends into the orders. Most of the guys in the warehouse helped themselves to parts for their cars; polish, oil, air and fuel filters, tie rod ends and radiator hoses. There were a few close calls but there were never any accusations. My thick set, fifty-something boss called me into his office and asked me to take two weeks holiday. He had some lame motivational cartoon posters on the wall and then relayed his philosophic attitude to work at me with a calm baritone voice.

"Steve, imagine this bucket here is full of water and all the employees in this company have their hand plunged into the water. The level rises and fills the bucket. Imagine if you took your hand out of that bucket. Do you think anyone would notice? The level would hardly drop." He looked me sternly in the eye to see if I had registered his meaning. I nodded and took two weeks paid holiday which I think was about $318.00 per week.

I went to the beach for a few days and returned to slough around Brisbane with my mates for a week. When I went back in to work I was handed my final 'redundancy pay' and was told that they were also letting other people in the warehouse go due to restructuring. That was supposed to make me feel better knowing I wasn't the only one, but I suspected that my boss had a spy or spies somewhere in the building. I left without as much as a tear being shed but some of the girls and guys gave me a cupcake with a candle in it wishing me the very best and 'sorry to see you go'. Some of us agreed to meet at the Hamilton Hotel that afternoon and proceeded to get stupidly pissed. By the time I managed to find my way home I still had my final pay-packet in my pocket and my notepad of poems and ditties.

'My naive attempt at entering the literati.'

After a surfing trip in the Maldives I came back with an idea to write a book.

I was paddling out with my brother-in-law at Chickens when he skimmed this sandal/scuff across the water towards me. I picked it up and looked inside to see a crab desperately clinging to the barnacles on the inside. There were other smaller crabs clinging on as well. I wondered how long they had been there. The tsunami that hit these islands in 2004 would have washed all sorts of detritus from the islands including this scuff and I thought that maybe the crab had been adrift for quite some time. We skimmed it around for a while showing all the other surfers. One of the smaller crabs jumped off and latched onto our surf guide's leg rope causing him to flick the scuff further out in the ocean. As I paddled towards it, I pushed it in front of a wave and after some minutes, watched it wash up on the shore of the island. Thus began 'Kontiki the Crab.'

Once home, I wrote a story about perseverance and determination and asked an illustrator to interpret my naïve stick drawings. She did a beautiful job of translating Kontiki into a cute crustacean character and I self-published and began distributing the book to schools newsagents and bookshops. It was really a sideline to my real job as a teacher at the time but this was my first foray into writing and publishing. Despite the cost of the exercise I made very little money from sales. It wasn't exactly an overnight sensation but the sales are still dribbling in.

I set up at bookstores in Caloundra and Buderim hoping to gain some momentum but I realised I wasn't cut out for the cutthroat world of hustling. I much preferred to just write.

'A bit of cash on the side...'

My wife and I set up a stall at Greasefest in Brisbane selling her handmade clothes and all sorts of odds and ends we'd collected over the years. I had Kontiki prominently displayed along with my old books and magazines, newspapers, memorabilia and collectibles.

I sold a box of "What Susan Did Next" novels to an older woman who had lost her entire collection in the 2011 floods. I'd bought the whole box for five dollars at a garage sale and was selling them, carefully wrapped, for five dollars each. She came back a second time and offered me thirty five for the whole box. Done! I sold a few copies of Kontiki and piles of old newspapers and comics. My wife sold her clothes and collectibles as the whole theme of Greasefest engulfed us. There were vintage cars and hot rods, rockabilly bands and young women dressed in their best fifties finery complete with arm and leg tattoos of Betty Boop and roses. They had all gone to a lot of trouble to look authentic and we had a fun day bringing home about seven hundred dollars in total.

We did other similar markets in Caloundra and Yandina with mixed success. The few garage sales we hosted earned us enough money to repair the fence and have some pocket money for a holiday to Barcelona. Do they count as jobs? We made money but weren't hired.

'Surviving on a student's income.'

When I was studying in Toowoomba I had several jobs which kept me afloat as a student. One of those was as director of The Recreation Council's new camp at Lake Perseverance near Crow's Nest. I was asked to co-ordinate a group of students to set up the opening day of the camp. Over the next few weeks I visited the site with students to allocate jobs for the big day and make sure everything went smoothly. The army built an abseiling wall and was on hand to help with the ropes and belaying. There were stalls of cupcakes and food, educational talks by environmentalists and fun activities for all the visiting children and parents. It was a huge success as many people from surrounding areas came to see the new camp opened. I was paid about three hundred dollars and the other students were paid about fifty dollars each for their efforts. We all received a certificate of thanks from the Rec council which went towards credit points for our studies.

On the morning of the opening I was at the camp before sunrise and, in the silence of the cool morning, was privileged to see two platypuses frolicking in the dam as I watched quietly from the jetty. The day was a huge success. I visited the site recently but it seemed to be abandoned although I was assured by a local that it was still used by school groups and sporting teams.

'Humility gives you power.'

One of the more permanent jobs I had while studying was waiting tables at the Mexican Cantina in Ruthven Street. Fernando, the owner, tall and thin, was from Mexico and was very particular about his food being authentic. He imported jalapenos and beans from Mexico and made corn chips from his own recipe at a factory in Brisbane.

Needless to say, it was popular and I was sometimes working three or four nights a week including Friday and Saturday nights. Most of the other staff waiting tables were students too and we were run off our feet. I enjoyed the atmosphere and being busy. All of the kitchen staff had been hand-selected by Fernando and he would go to great lengths to train them in the art of preparing authentic Mexican food. To this day, I have not had better. There was a classical guitarist from the Uni who played on busy nights and I thought she was talented and gorgeous. I approached her after work one night and asked if she could give me lessons. She agreed and I had my first lesson with her on the following Tuesday. I was nervous but she was encouraging and did not charge me much knowing I was also a student. She was patient and gave me practice songs for the week which I tried to make a good fist of (my left hand resembled a fist when I played). On the third week I turned up for my lesson at her house and saw a strange car in the driveway with its lights on. I reached into the unlocked vehicle and turned the lights off. I knocked at the door but received no answer. I could hear splashing and then a male voice and then a female voice laughing. I realised I had walked in on Kari and her 'friend' and left realising she had forgotten. There were no more lessons after that as she left me a note on the door saying she was moving to Brisbane.

At the restaurant, Fernando was giving me more nights than I could handle and I had to 'appear to be' studying. I managed to get a night or two playing guitar in Kari's place and continued waiting tables on the busy nights. Fernando looked after me and I always had huge take home nachos with all the trimmings. It kept me afloat for more than a year and I appreciated Fernando's generosity; thank you Fernando.

'If only they could see themselves.'

I also worked at the Uni club which was called 'The Club' serving behind the bar on nights when I wasn't at the Cantina. Students would pour in at about seven, drink, dance to crappy tunes like the Bus Stop and Nutbush City Limits trying to hook up with whomever they could and then stagger home to attempt a drunken and embarrassing re-enactment of procreation. The money was actually quite good and I got knock off drinks and a six pack of my favourite beer at the time, 'Tooheys Old'. One night these two young girls walked in looking very sheepish and unsure of themselves and I asked for ID which they produced and I served them a drink. They proceeded to get blind drunk and on the way out one of them turned to me while I was cleaning up and said, "I'm gonna suck you dry", with a slurred speech and wide rolling eyes. I nodded and said, jokingly, 'OK' but her friend dragged her out the door before she collapsed. I said under my breath, 'your mother would be proud of you at this moment' and laughed at my boss who was standing nearby. He smiled and continued mopping the floor.

There were many of those laughable moments at the club, including some of my fellow mature-age students, who slowly deteriorated over each night while their debauched attempts at finding a lovely girl to escort home frittered into another beer. I was happy to be on the other side of the bar and earning money rather than spending it. I was five or six years older than most of the students and realised I had been given a second chance to pursue my dream of becoming a teacher. I was about eighteen months away from achieving that dream. I was working three jobs, studying, renovating our new/old house, losing weight (from 86 kilos to 73 eventually) and getting very fit, cycling, playing basketball and golf.

> 'Remain in a good mood and be cheerful despite your reeling brain.'
>
> (Meher Baba)

The Meher Baba sect found its way to Brisbane in the form of an Indian clothing import company in Fortitude Valley. Steven and his wife were members of the sect (although they were both German?) and I managed to get a job in the warehouse because of my mum's contacts in Baxter Street where she worked. I was the assistant storeman to an Irishman named Michael. He was a genuinely good natured man with a thick accent from a southern Irish county. We worked well together moving fuchsia and yellow coloured clothes around the warehouse and stacking and packing orders to be picked up. I rarely saw the owner Steven or his wife in their mezzanine office and they trusted Michael and I to do what we were paid to do. There was never a dull moment; well actually, there was a lot of downtime because of our efficiency at getting most things done in the morning. As soon as the boss left, we had a cup of tea.

One day Michael was addressing an 'Air Mail' letter to his mum in Ireland. The address went something like this. To Ma Flaherty, (not their real name) C/O Big Jim at the Cork Pub, C/O little Jim (presumably at the bar) C/O Aunt Mary and little Robert, Cork. In case you're wondering, C/O meant 'care of'. There was no physical address written on the letters but somehow they always managed to get to her.

The pay was pretty ordinary but I enjoyed meeting Michael and gaining new skills in an industry which I had never imagined would generate so much money. Those cheesecloth pants and shirts were everywhere. They were cheap, colourful clothing and anyone who wore or sold them was mostly oblivious to the fact that they were supporting the Meher Baba sect either willingly or unwittingly.

I had been looking through the Courier Mail jobs classifieds and got an interview in Queen Street in the city just as I heard that the warehouse was closing down and Michael was going back to Ireland. Thanks for all your sage advice Michael; you were a blessing amongst all the phonies I had to deal with on a daily basis. Craic agus ceol.

Many years later, my wife and I met a woman who is the daughter of a famous American film producer (she never said who it was). We had become close friends before we learned that she was going to meet Meher Baba and have her children blessed by him. Apparently, at the meeting, Baba told her that her blonde-haired young daughter was very special and he chose her from the crowd of thousands to be blessed by him. Needless to say, the mum was blessed too and she came back with fascinating stories of sudden enlightenment after the blessing.

The woman remarried twice and had three more children while her eldest blonde-haired daughter joined the army; so much for the blessings of Meher Baba. I never shared my experience working in the warehouse of Meher Baba with them but I gained a new insight into what I had been doing all those years ago. In my case, Meher paid me and I never donated a cent to his cause although there was always a clearly labelled donation box at the entrance to the warehouse. I'm sure he meant well; initially.

'Milk from a stone.'

Custom Credit Corporation was a huge finance company set up in Queen Street in Brisbane in the old post office building. The company no longer exists because eventually it self-imploded due to massive corruption. There were over three floors of desks and phones trying to sell credit to those who couldn't afford it and to those who were rich enough to exploit it. The position of collections officer had come up and I had experience. The same three questions magically appeared; National Anthem? Do you drink? And do you play sport?

"Waltzing Matilda; yes, I enjoy a cold beer on a hot day and I play touch footy," I said almost robotically but then added, "But I don't mind a nice port near the fire on a cool winter day such as this." The manager looked at me with a raised face and arms strung up behind his head in a relaxed manner saying, "Yes, 'Grandfathers' for lunch would be nice." He looked out the window and then said, "I'll call you Steve; I have several other interviews to conduct today so, I'll be in touch." He stood and proffered his hand, smiling professionally and letting me know by his facial expressions and stronger aftershave that he was the boss.

I sauntered my cheap suit (which wasn't really a suit, just nylon pants, cotton shirt and rayon tie) out the door and decided I was confident enough to go and buy some decent clothes and shoes and get a haircut that suited the modern young businessman's life.

I'd saved some money from my previous job and had enrolled at the Stock Exchange to study a new course called 'Futures' and was attending night classes in business law and economics.

The next day I received the call that I had been selected to start on Monday at eight precisely. Lucky I bought that new suit on the Thursday because I wore it to my brother's wedding on the Saturday (yes it matched the other four groomsmen) and then proceeded on the Monday, to parade the slightly sweaty, pale blue suit into the offices of Custom Credit Corporation brandishing my five week old moustache and a distinctly Spanish sounding surname. At the time, 'Blue Stratos' was the preferred assault on everyone's olfactory senses. I must have looked like Guido the Mexican pimp (or drug dealer) but I was shown to my desk and introduced to some of my colleagues who (ironically) included Dave and Alan. I sort of gravitated towards them and we spent many a drunken night singing at the Embassy Hotel and creating tontines 'regarding a rare bottle of 1966 Dow Port' that have not yet been fulfilled . It's still in the public trust office awaiting our deaths; or not?

There was a very fat Greek man in the cubicle in front of me named George who seemed to be eating some kind of falafel all the time; a skinny hyperactive guy named Carl with streaked, styled and gelled hair and squeaky voice was to my right, and then, a huge bank of typists and receptionists behind where I sat. The dividers between each section were low so everyone could see everyone, except the bosses had offices with doors. My accounts were from L to N which was still quite substantial but I was being eased into the office and began making calls to people who owed money. It was an art. With suit coat draped across the back of my swivelling office chair and loosened tie, I would talk to people of all different cultures and communities. Most were honest people who couldn't afford the payments and made promises to part-pay when they could afford it. The option was repossession which meant they would have to pay for the repossession costs and then be without a vehicle. The company was ruthless in its approach despite the fact that they were losing money as well. The company could afford to write off huge amounts from the bottom end against the profits they were making from car companies and businesses that were thriving. The little man always suffered. I was the one trying to get milk from a stone on the bottom line of humanity.

Apart from cajoling people into making a payment on their overdue lease, I would occasionally be asked to go out into the field, cold calling on the most 'behind' accounts.

The company car was an eggplant coloured Ford Telstar front wheel drive with balding tyres. At some point they upgraded to a white version of the same model car which had been purloined somewhere amongst all the scams the company was reputed to have perpetrated on car yards in Brisbane. When the hammer came down everyone rushed for cover.

There was a sudden need to hide bucks from the tax department before things got really serious and they had to be accountable. Millions were written off and 'missing' as the shadows of the company melted into overseas ventures and markets that were 'emerging'.

Every time I drove out of the underground carpark with my

valise of documents I felt apprehensive about what I would encounter. I lit a cigarette, as everyone did in those days, and wound down the window holding the cigarette near the open window to reduce the smell in the car. It still smelled of the previous driver's Marlboro or Dunhill or whatever and the ashtray was overflowing to the point where it was easier to flick the butt out the window (yes, we did that in those days, oops). On occasions, I would pull up at a public bin to empty the ashtray, only to leave my own butts in there at the end of the day as I parked the car for the next un-suspecting collections officer. I wonder if fat George sat in this seat…

I still truly believed that people were innately good and could be reasoned with. That was my approach; knocking on doors that wouldn't open despite the tirade that was going on inside. Thirtyish something stressed women with five children trying to cover for their husband's incompetence at staying out of jail. I was truly sympathetic. They were angry.

"I'll give you some of my shopping money, he'll be out on Monday and we can afford petrol to get the kids to school." She was pleading and I accepted the measly twenty dollars she offered to cover the three hundred dollar deficit on their HQ wagon.

"We'll pay the rest on the next payday," she said obviously distraught at her situation. I said that would be a 'promise to pay' and if she honoured it, we wouldn't repossess the car. Back at the office my boss saw different and said, "Call Pinkertons and get the car." I was incredulous.

"She made a 'promise to pay'. We have to give them a chance to honour that payment before we take their car, surely?"

"Get the car!"

I walked to my desk and phoned Pinkertons who arranged for the pickup on Monday morning at five thirty. I was there on the day handing her paperwork and watching the repossessions guy hitching up the car amidst her protests. "How do I get my kids to school and do the shopping and pick up my husband from prison you bastard. I told you I would pay and you said you wouldn't take the car, you #$*%$^@ bastard." I felt horrible having agreed not to take the car and now, to keep my job, I had to take her car. All the kids were lined up on the balcony watching their vehicle being towed away while their distressed mother swore with increasing displeasure and indignation.

They owed $900 on the car and were $300 dollars behind on previous payments. The repossession cost $600 and the car was auctioned for $200. The company wrote off the debt of $900, paid Pinkertons $600 and got $200 back on the sale of the vehicle for a total loss of $1300 dollars while paying me a measly $80 dollars a day for my efforts. No wonder they went under very quickly just before Keating said something about the 'recession' we had to have.

On another of my outings to catch non-payers at home, I pulled up at an address in Morningside and knocked on the front door. Hearing sounds from inside but not being addressed at the front door I skipped around to the back door. A man greeted me coldly. "Are you Frank Williams?" (Not his real name). I was to serve a summons on him to appear in court for defaulting on his payments. He glared at me and reached for an axe just near the doorway. "If you don't fuck off I'll set the dogs on yer!" he said, brandishing the axe in both hands. I threw the paper at him as he whistled his Dobermans into action. I ran around the house in record time, hurdled the wooden/wire fence and ran up onto the roof of my car as the dogs came bounding over the fence baying and trying to climb the car with scratching claws. I yelled into the neighbourhood, "Whose dogs are these? Someone call the police!" Several neighbours emerged to look at me standing on top of the car in slippery plastic heels trying to avoid the gnarling dogs at my feet. There was a whistle from the house and the dogs retreated faithfully over the fence. One of the neighbours clapped and gave me the thumbs up. I'm sure the owner of the dogs was watching from inside, smiling.

Once back inside the car with heart pounding like an Olympic sprinter I checked my fingers and shoes and paperwork. I was sweaty but reasonably unscathed. I breathed and drove off.

The next job that day was at Birkdale for a young guy who bought a motorbike on hire purchase and hadn't paid for three months. Every contact I'd had with his dad had been evasive. His dad said he'd gone to Tasmania for work as a plumber. I asked him to consider his son's debt as he was the guarantor on the loan but he resisted and said he didn't know where the bike was or where his son was now living. He was evasive to say the least. I had chased this kid around the neighbourhood on several visits and this was no different. As I drove down the street I saw him in the distance and he took off into the surrounding neighbourhood with me pushing the Telstar a bit beyond its real capacity. He disappeared around this corner and there was an older woman on her balcony pretending to be non-chalant. I paused, smelling the motorbike fuel and asked her, "Hey, have you seen a kid on a motorbike through here?" She nodded negative dragging on her cigarette and was way too convincing to be just standing on the balcony at that time. I looked at my documents and realised it was his grandmother's place. There was still smoke coming from under the garage door for fucks sake Grandma!

I drove off sheepishly pretending I was giving up, only retracing my steps back to his father's place ten minutes later after a sandwich and a think.

Just by chance, as I pulled up at the residence, I saw the father on his balcony talking to his daughter who had her back to me. She didn't know I was there. I had visited the father on previous occasions and he recognised me and tried to warn his daughter not to say anything. It was too late. "He's up the end of the road waiting for us to take him to Doug's" (his boss I had deduced). She was loading the car with her brother's stuff and her father was waving wildly at her and yelling at me. I jumped back in the car and drove to the end of the street near the mangroves where a young man was pacing cautiously at my approach.

"Do you know where I could find Jeffrey Smith?"(Not his real name) I asked knowing it was him. He looked sheepishly through the window of the car and said, "No, but I can get him a message."

"Tell him that the federal police are looking for him and that if he doesn't relinquish his bike he will go to court and be liable for all the costs." He looked at me and agreed he would tell his friend. I drove out to the main road and waited for the sister's car to emerge onto the busy street south and followed it about five kilometres to his boss's house where they quickly closed the garage to hide the car. That was part of my cold call day and I had no idea how effective or ineffective I was until the next business day when I heard that the Doberman protected/axe man had back paid his debt to avoid court and the kid had ridden his bike into the Mount Gravatt branch and gave it up. He wasn't in Tasmania after all and his dad and grandma paid the arrears in order to avoid another visit from me or someone similar. I must have effectively communicated my message at that point in time.

One of the various visits to the Boggo Road prison sticks with me. I had a letter from work stating my official business and was led to the gate where I was going to interview a prisoner about a missing car. He wasn't in there for stealing the car but he knew something about it. As I flicked my wallet open to show my ID to the guard, a Gillette shaving cartridge, which I had put there to remind me to buy more, fell out on the ground at my feet. He looked at me and said to his colleague in a loud voice, "Mr Chill, we'll have this prisoner behind the wall," or something to that effect implying that I was perhaps smuggling in a razor for someone's suicide or escape, I thought.

We sat opposite each other with a very thick resin/plastic screen between us and I tried to ask him about the missing car. He was barely literate and seemed dazed about who I was.

"No, my uncle (who owned the caryard) gave it to me. He took it back, for his girlfriend. I dunnow where it is."

"Where is your uncle?" After a few wags of the head, he looks at me.

"I dunnow", he replied. My time was being wasted. It was obvious his uncle had set him up and he was serving time as a patsy to a much more sinister plot. Poor kid was a victim of someone else's greed and his uncle may never pay for it. We never found the car.

On another visit to Boggo Road, I managed to get inside and walked through to the main guard box where I asked for Tom Murray (not his real name). The guard pointed to a jockey sized man sweeping the concrete.

"Are you Tom?" He nodded and I gave him the summons to appear in court. He seemed relatively calm and approachable.

"Yeah, I get out next mundy and I'll pay $600 for the car cos I'll need it to go to work and drop the kids at school." He smiled at me as though everything in his life was good even though he had been served a summons in prison while serving time for a completely unrelated incident. I gave him a card with my number on it and he tucked it into his top pocket. I scanned the guardhouse and cells beyond, which were dark, noisy and eerie to say the least.

"You'll still have to go to court for the other lease you had on that wrecked car."

"Yeah, it'll be fine mate. I'll send you some money when I get out." He smiled and shook my hand and went back to sweeping while whistling loudly. On the way out, I checked the layout of the prison and suddenly realised its' archaic infrastructure of brick and concrete. It is now a museum of sorts which you can visit. Lots of stories came out of there.

The day after his release date, Tom came into the city office with his wife and paid two hundred and fifty dollars (not the agreed $600) just to keep the wolves from the door. If you made an effort to pay, you could avoid further action from the company. Tom and his wife were very cordial and made promises to pay another amount next week. I accepted and waved them off. When my boss heard of the payment plan he said...

"Get the car!"

"They're nice people, he just got out of prison and they have children. C'mon, at least give them a chance. I gave them my word. How is it going to look now if I go back on my word?"

"You should have checked with me before making that deal. You don't represent the company policy. They are defaulters and always have been. How do you think this company makes money to pay your wages? Get the car." He turned and walked to his office while I called the repo agents. Fortunately, I wasn't present at that particular repossession but I did get an abusive call from Tom's wife the next day. I had to insist that the decision came from higher up and I apologised profusely while she slammed the phone down in my ear.

Not one of my favourite moments in my forty jobs. Needless to say, Alan, Dave and I got pissed at the Embassy and sang into the night. Actually Dave couldn't sing as he had two tin ears.

On Tuesday nights after work I walked to the stock exchange with my leather briefcase (which was a 21st birthday gift from my uncle and aunt) for my 'Futures' lesson and on Thursday nights I walked to another old sandstone building to listen to these energetic men who were 'bastions of business and business law'. These guys were the gurus of making money at the time and the crowd consisted of professionals in the industry, lawyers, bankers and everything in between including myself and all the other young wannabes. We were all supposed to listen to their sage advice and then ask intelligent questions afterwards. There were always graphs projected on the whiteboard and they spoke in a language that was way too idiosyncratic for me to understand. Numbers never were my strong point and sometimes I would glaze over and look at the gathered crowd trying to work out who was who. One particular night we arrived for the business law lecture and Dave came with me to see what it was all about. Dave was rapt in the whole scene.

It was about six o'clock before the presenter appeared, apparently just from work, took off his jacket and spoke for about three minutes before he froze, fell unceremoniously from the low stage and hit the deck unconscious. Everyone stood with concerned murmurs to see his two colleagues attending to him and loosening his tie and wiping his forehead. Once we saw he was in good hands, we politely left and went across the road for a drink.

"If that's what it takes to earn money by the time your thirty, then I'd rather be poor," I said to Dave. "I don't want to work myself to death like that. He was just totally exhausted and probably dehydrated and stressed and had a poor diet and …" Dave nodded and sipped his beer. "Yeah, poor bastard; he looked like he'd recovered though by the time we left."

"How old do reckon he is Dave?"

"About thirty or so," he said sipping more beer.

"I reckon he was only late twenties but looked older because of his stress." It was a real thing in those days. Many people in that industry just burned out trying to chase the elusive dollar while all those magic-family-moments in their lives slid past them. It didn't help that all our clothes in those days were hot nylon, including underwear.

The next day at work I was given a new task totally unrelated to my job.

The CCC big boss, Wayne, who'd interviewed me, was keen on entering a touch footy team in the local finance competition which included banks and financial institutions in general.

"We've got a few gun players in the building Steve. Do you think you could organise some CCC (Custom Credit Corporation) shirts and put us in for the Wednesday night comp?"

"Sure, I'll organise the shirts and look at the team before we play. Are you playing Wayne?"

"Yes, I'd like a run every now and then. I'd like to be there for the games. Check out Brett in loans downstairs. He's a gun player." I nodded and went about my business of procuring our team shirts with a CCC logo in red like the company colours. A friend of my brother's volunteered to print the shirts and when they came back they had leaked and dripped like blood down from the three C's. I couldn't believe it. I had paid good money for the shirts but refused to pay for the dodgy screen printing. When my boss saw them he imploded but we didn't have time to change as the game was that night. My chances of promotion waned considerably (and that was before his lovely secretary seduced me).

Once assembled at the field I handed out the shirts which looked like blood was dripping down their chest. Some of the players actually thought it was cool as everyone's shirt was a different badly printed version of Dracula's napkin.

We had a formidable team and were in the top three for the first few weeks. Brett, from loans was indeed a great strategic player and we linked up well in moves we'd learned playing Rugby League. Wayne subbed on and played for a few minutes each game and cheered us from the sideline as 'The Bloody C's'. "C'mon, you bloody C's."

During the semi-finals, Brett dived to tag a player and landed awkwardly on his shoulder. We were one all with the NAB. Calmly, he came over to me with a dislocated shoulder and I told him to go off.

"I'm not leaving the field Steve, you know what to do." I could see the pain on his face and advised him to ask the first aid guy who was a volunteer. "Just do it." I did know what to do and reluctantly stuck my fist in his armpit and pulled his arm back down over the shoulder socket. He winced and returned to the game making clever plays that sucked up time til the hooter. Brett was in a shoulder sling for two weeks before we made the final against AGC. He'd missed one game.

The 'bloody shirts' had become well known in the competition and we had a decent crowd at the Grand Final. AGC, (who I had previously worked for), had hired gun players from far afield in the company or some boss's nephew who was an Australian junior champion and this sprinter from Canberra who did not even work for the company. The betting between bosses and everyone else at the game would have been enough to clear ten overdue accounts at the company. We did a credible job but were outclassed 3-2; so ended the 'bloody shirts' of CCC. Needless to say we got pissed on Wayne's expense account that night. Some of the girls from the office came to the game wearing the spare 'bloody' CCC shirts and cheered us on.

Katrina and Carol joined us for drinks and took Brett and I to a party in Red Hill afterwards still dressed in our grass-stained stinky 'blood-shirts' and touch boots. That was the first time I'd heard Brian Ferry's 'Sensation'. I was instantly hooked and told Katrina to play it again. She kicked one of her flatmates out of the main bed (which had no sheets) and we proceeded to get naked and drunkenly frolic around under a coverless feather doona. Brett had too much pain in his shoulder to party so Carol took him to her house to soothe him. By early morning I had found my shorts and shirt and called a taxi. I left without my boots and socks which Katrina ceremoniously handed to me on Monday morning in front of the whole office. Needless to say I copped a fair amount of ribbing from Alan and Dave.

"Oooh, Steve? What have we been up to?" asked the skinny, nervous guy with gelled hair.

"I left them at the footy ground and she was kind enough to return them,' was my defensive answer. No-one believed for a minute. I did link up with Katrina at the work Christmas party on a boat in the Brisbane River. We got off the boat at the first stop available and by the time we got to her place she was vomiting from the taxi and delirious. It was one of those nights where I held her hair back from the toilet bowl so she didn't vomit into it; too much champagne. Once she was asleep I caught a taxi home ready for the Christmas break and visiting family. I ceased to attend the stock exchange course and other lectures through pure apathy. I really wasn't cut out for the competitive world of 'high finance' or was it 'low finance?' I ploughed on for a few more months enjoying the inner city night life after work.

Alan, Dave and I purchased a rare bottle of 1966 Dow port from the cellar master at the Brisbane Club who I had met when I worked there. It cost us $81 dollars at the time and we placed it in a sealed metal cash box with masking tape around the outside containing our signatures. The guy at the public trust office registering the box said...

"Hey, you guys have got some of that rare wine that's going around?" His eyes went wide but we assured him it was nothing to do with wine.

The deal was a tontine, as you know, which means that the last man standing would claim the port on producing the death certificates of the other two. I have my doubts that it is still there. Another plan at that time was to auction the bottle for a thousand bucks in 2000 when it would be 34 years old or crack it and drink it if we didn't get our auction price. It's now 55 years old. Hmmm!

Over the years since, I have had one contact with each of those men I worked with at CCC. Dave, at the time, was an accountant with his own firm and Alan was trying to marry into wealth using his Bing Crosby, private-school-boy charm to avoid spending his eccentric grandmother's inheritance. He was raised by her in an 'Old-English-School' privilege but chose to go out and work with the 'plebs' as he called us. Alan was funny and entertaining as well as quite a good crooner. We laughed a lot about ridiculous stories we'd shared.

At the Empire Hotel he would always lead the song and ask the piano player for 'New York, New York' at least three times in a night. Dave was a little more reserved and preferred to watch Alan and I botch the lyrics only to come back stronger on the chorus. Dave mouthed the words with a wide grin on his face and usually left early saying, "You two are nuts."

Some nights Alan and I would each rent a room at the Sheraton and invite whoever round for drinks and 'unstated' shenanigans. We drank and sang at the bar and then took the party to one of the rooms until it was obvious who was going to end up with whom.

A lovely Greek girl I met in the bar downstairs spent the night with me. In the morning, when I was leaving at about eight o'clock, she said to me...

"I'm never going to see you again am I?"

"What's your phone number?" She paused, said the number and then tried to write it down for me.

"I have a good memory," and I repeated the six digit number to her. After a brief kiss, I left her to enjoy the free breakfast in the tenth story room overlooking the city and made my sad and un-showered way home. The next day I phoned her and she was surprised that I had remembered her number. I asked her if she wanted to go out somewhere on Friday and mentioned a band playing at the Orient Hotel. She paused and said, "I have a boyfriend."

"Ok," I said, also pausing. "No pressure. I'm going out with my sister and her friends anyway, I'd like you to come," another pause on her end. She said, "Ok, I'll meet you there."

"Great, I'll be the one at the door who looks like me." She laughed and we agreed to meet on Friday at the Orient at eight.

Alan and Dave had also come along for the happy hour but Dave disappeared early on when the first band started playing. Alan was scouting the room for anyone who reeked of eccentric breeding. He quickly found his people and proceeded to astonish them with his crooning version of 'New York, New York'. My sister, cousin and some of their friends had come into town to see this band I had recommended and were well and truly primed by the time the Greek girl appeared at the entrance looking for me. I'd been expecting her and was constantly looking towards the door. She was wearing a loose-fitting olive green top and tight jeans; she spotted me but waved me off. I walked towards her but she gave the distinct impression that I wasn't to approach her. She gravitated towards the band and embraced a Greek-looking guy with gold chains around his neck. I got it; it was her boyfriend who was a friend of the band. At one point he left her and went outside with his gang, probably for a snort. She looked at me from across the room and smiled.

She sidled up to me at the bar and explained her situation with the boyfriend and the band.

My sister bumped in between us at the bar and introduced herself cheerily.

"Hi, I'm Lisa, Stephen's sister."

"Nice to meet you Lisa," she said extending her hand but looking at me. After some homogenised pleasantries, the Greek girl left and I never saw her again.

"Who was that Stephen?" Lisa asked with pure innocence and a few drinks under her belt.

"Just a woman I met through work," I lied. I watched the Greek girl walk away wondering if she was really going to be OK. Besides, why would she have spent the night with me? I hope you're alright lovely Greek girl and you have had a fulfilling and prosperous life.

There were many nights at the Sheraton where Alan and I would drink til the bar closed and then go up to his room and drain the mini-bar and then move on to my room and drain the mini-bar until someone either passed out or was dragged to their room by several others including Carol, Katrina and a young Italian girl, Marina, who somehow found our company amusing. She was a big built girl with a lovely smile like Sophia Loren, and she could dance.

Marina joined us on our jaunts around town and to the 'Underground' night club in Milton which eventually became the Spaghetti Emporium. The old building was originally a flour mill but, as a massive nightclub, it was great for dancing and socialising well after midnight. Friday nights were always packed and my sister and cousin used to join us on the dance floor. My favourite song to dance to at the time was "Girlfriend" by Talking Heads.

Reality hit back at work on Monday. I had a repo planned for ten o'clock at a property in Aspley which was quite rural in those days. This guy had defaulted on payments for his V8 Fairlane. I met the 'Pinkertons' guys at the gate with the paperwork and after unsuccessfully being allowed in, they proceeded to cut the chain, swing the big gates open and reversed their tow-truck up to the car. The owner's Rottweilers were going nuts and I stayed well back. The Pinkertons guys had seen it all before a million times and they were tough. One carried a hammer, the other a tyre iron. They were not afraid of the dogs.

"If that dog touches me I'll smash his head in with this hammer." He looked defiantly at the man who was now brandishing a shotgun from the doorway. I froze and tried to melt into the background. He looked in my direction, then at the other two and called the dogs inside.

"If you touch that car, which is on my property..." he waved the gun vaguely at the ground.

"...And what? You gonna shoot me and go to jail? I don't think so," said the hefty Pinkerton.

They hooked up the car and gestured for me to give him the paperwork.

"And you're the prick who rang me the other day," he said resting the gun against the inside door and leering at me. I walked towards him keeping my eye on the dogs which were still snarling and salivating. He snatched the paperwork from me and turned inside. The Pinkertons had waited til I was safe out the door and walking towards the gate. As they drove out with the Fairlane attached, the driver leaned out at me and said, "You looked like you were gonna shit yourself for a minute there Steve." They both chuckled and I replied, "I'm not so sure I haven't," giving them a nervous smile.

That night on the news, police were called to a residence in Aspley where shots had been fired and they had arrested a man for questioning. The TV reporters had caught the moment he was being arrested and it was 'our man who used to own a Fairlane' being manhandled to a Police car.

For years after, I always imagined one of those people remembering my name and coming looking for me. My signature was all over the paperwork. Now, those things are gone and forgotten by two generations, the company went under owing money to creditors about the same time Christopher Skase escaped to Majorca. I worked with lots of interesting people, learned new skills, had loads of fun and earned enough money to buy a house with my girlfriend, ironically, in Aspley.

As things go in finance companies, I was let go, being the last one hired and some lame excuse about the percentages on my books. I knew they were good and thought maybe it was my soft approach to helping people pay their debts. C'est la vie. We all got pissed at the Empire Hotel that night and I rarely saw any of them again.

'A bit of fun in the sun...'

Back in cooler climes in Toowoomba, when I was studying, I managed to get into a busking competition in the main street during the 'Carnival of Flowers'. Well, it wasn't really a competition but there were varying degrees of prizes on offer and we got to keep our busking money. At the time I was learning saxophone and played 'Amazing Grace' reasonably well enough for people to recognise. When I got sick of that I would pick up the guitar and go through my repertoire of classical and jazzy sort of tunes. Then I would have a break and juggle for ten minutes or so. Every hour we would have to move to a different spot in the city centre around Margaret Street. The two judges were an elderly lady and a young girl who could have been her granddaughter. They would pause and make appreciative and encouraging comments while writing down their impressions of each performer. There were whole families dressed in country uniforms and hats, unicyclists, flautists and other ensembles from the music department of the Uni, magicians and clowns.

At the end of the day the country family band deservedly won the major prize. Second went to a young girl singing and playing guitar and third were just as deserving with a lively cello and flute duo. I went home with twenty seven dollars of busking money and a smile on my face. I love the Carnival of Flowers. I love flowers for that matter.

After Uni on the Tuesday I received a cheque in the mail from the organisers of the busking competition to say that I had won

$100 for being the most versatile performer on the day. Stoked! It was one of forty endeavours where I earned money but I certainly didn't consider that a job. It was fun and I met a lot of nice people in that spring of 1987?

> 'Be content with what you have;
> rejoice in the way things are.
> When you realise there is nothing lacking,
> the whole world belongs to you.'
>
> (Lao-tzu)

When I was three months shy of eighteen, I went to Sunshine Beach looking for work. My Uncle had kindly asked if I wanted to be his apprentice but I couldn't imagine myself as a plumber. He offered for me to go and get some experience with his future son-in-law Reg who was a builder. I'd already tried the building sites at first point Noosa to no avail and ended up living in my uncle's shack near the beach with Reg. He was building a house in Park Crescent just 100 metres up the road. I was to be his willing apprentice and eventually moved into the incomplete house with him, although I felt more like a slave working for food and accommodation, which was meagre to say the least.

If the surf was good in the morning, we would surf for an hour or so and then get back to the house to dig foundations and paint and hump all sorts of building material into the two-storied house. I didn't even get paid at first, just getting meals and sparse accommodation in a cold concrete bedroom with no hot water; and surf. I didn't give a damn. I was living the dream that so many of us had talked about in school. Nothing else seemed free to me but this was a choice I'd made. This was where I wanted to be, despite the long unadventurous hours of working on a site where great music was playing loud and we had access to a billy three times a day; most of the time it was just the two of us. Reg was a couple of years older than me and spent an inordinate amount of time with my cousin (understandably). Sometimes, I'd scrounge a few bucks from him to go out and have a beer. I relied on the kindness of strangers at times when I would just not drink because I couldn't afford it; someone always offered to buy me a drink; Thankyou strangers. Thankyou Alison for that wonderful night at the Noosa Surf club.

On some early mornings, the surf would be classic-all-time glassy four to six foot barrels on a little bank to the south. All the locals and our friends joined us in the perfect conditions for as long as it lasted, sometimes up to four hours. And the next day was shrouded in mist but just as perfect and grey-green like you've never seen. I shared a barrel with my friend Andrew on one wave and we hooted and paddled back out for the next ten perfect silvery-green waves.

It lasted three days and we were exhausted from paddling, ate a lot of bananas, barbecued steak and cheap steamed veggies and slept soundly. Needless to say, we didn't get much work done and then suddenly it started to rain.

We were stuck in the house with Alan Parson's 'I Robot' blaring, a few billy teas and occasionally going for the afternoon surf in the rain at the incoming tide. There were lots of visitors on weekends including some of Reg's friends, their girlfriends and their girlfriend's girlfriends. They were all a couple of years older than me, but all beautiful in their own way.

Being just an apprentice in this world of cool surfer dudes

meant I didn't really have a chance for romance. I was just in the background watching and laughing at their antics. Occasionally, one of them would notice me sitting on the perimeters and ask me about the surf and give me a beer despite the fact that I was underage at the time. I willingly accepted.

Early starts were killer in the middle of winter. I only had one blanket and very few clothes which consisted of surf brand t-shirts, boardies, thongs and a cheap pair of Dunlop KT26 joggers. Sometimes I would dig foundations, sometimes paint and other times held plaster sheeting up while it was being tacked. Then one day, Reg fell from outside while putting up the balcony. A bird swooped him and as he ducked to avoid contact, lost his footing and fell awkwardly. His tool belt had swung around in front of him causing the hammer and nail bag to punch into his left shoulder. I saw it happen in slow motion, and, powerless to do anything I ran down to him. He was groaning and holding his shoulder lying on the ground. "I'll call the ambulance," I said. He dislodged his belt and stood shakily.

"No, I'll be right, just get me to the ute and you can drive to the hospital (which was twenty minutes away in Tewantin). I found the keys, and tried to get him into the white Ford ute.

"Wait, pack me one before we go," he smiled weakly at me and I ran inside, packed one and brought it to him in the car. After a few attempts at lighting it he managed to suck in a fair amount of smoke and then handed me the remnants saying, "Finish it." I did and then proceeded to drive to Tewantin. He pushed a cassette into the Clarion; Robin Trower's 'Long Misty Days' played as he nursed his shoulder quietly the whole time while

I was becoming increasingly paranoid about my speed and judging distances. Needless to say we made it and he sat in the emergency for about an hour before he was seen. He handed me some money and told me to go and get some food and go home. He would ring me later. 'Yes boss', I thought. I was still affected by the imbibement as I drove home in the twilight getting the feel of the car and the music blaring from the speaker behind my head.

I stopped at Sunshine Beach Junction and ordered a pizza from the classic 'Marios'. Best pizza on the planet, that was nearest to me at the time.

Fifteen minutes later, I was driving for Sunshine Beach trying to stuff a piece of pizza into my mouth, while changing the column shift gear from first to second with my greasy hand when I spot these two figures walking along the road with their thumbs out for a lift.

I dropped the pizza on the box, clutch in and slowed down just past them watching in the mirror as they hurried to the car. I leaned over and wound the window down.

A tallish girl with frizzy dark hair and big mischievous brown eyes stuck her head through the window and said, "We're going to Sunrise." The other girl was blonde and somewhat shorter. She peered in at me. I said, "I'm going to Sunshine. I'll drop you near the road".

They must have smelled the pizza, hurriedly opened the door and scrunched into the three-seater front of the ute nursing the pizza on their laps. They were both grinning from ear to ear and looking at me as I pulled out onto the road. Less than a kilometre up the road I slowed down to drop them off. "So, what are you doing tonight?" asked the frizzy-haired girl beaming a goofy smile at me. The little blonde looked expectantly with her crystal blue eyes.

"My boss is in the hospital and I have to go and pick him up when he rings."

"What happened?"

"He fell off the balcony; he's getting x-rays I think. I'm just going back to the house we're building to eat and wait for the phone call." I really did look and sound seventeen at this point and was barely tall enough to see over the dashboard without sitting up tall and compromising my reach to the pedals.

"Do you want us to come and wait with you? We're only a walk from where we're staying, and that pizza smells good," said the blonde girl who was now suddenly hungry or, more likely, had the munchies. "By the way, I'm Di," said the blonde, "and this is…" she paused and looked at her frizzy haired friend who decided to call herself 'Rhea'. They both laughed raucously at their joke which took me a few seconds to register. "I'm Stephen."

"Ok, as long as we leave some for Reg, I guess." I pulled the car back onto the road, drove a total of 750 metres and pulled into the driveway of the half built house on Park Crescent.

Once I tidied up the work site a bit in the darkness I led the girls into the house and found the light switch. They descended on the pizza and raided beers from the fridge while I was cleaning up the kitchen. I put a cassette of 'Dire Straits' on. They were giggling and thanking me now they knew my name. "Thanks Stephen, this house is awesome. Can I have a look upstairs?" They both looked at me with wide-eyed expectation; a piece of pizza in one hand and a stubby in the other.

"Just be careful of all the stuff on the floor," I warned.

As they went upstairs, I briefly showered in cold water and changed into my day old jeans, my least used T-shirt and a black Golden Breed hoody, hoping to smell better than I should have. I used some of Reg's aftershave before I emerged from the freezing bathroom even though I didn't really need to shave.

The phone rang. Reg said they were keeping him in overnight and would call me tomorrow. That was it. He hung up and I had no idea about the extent of his injuries. He reminds me now of the character played by Daniel Day Lewis in 'There will be Blood'; deadpan!

I ate the rest of my abandoned piece of pizza and cracked the second last beer to wash it down. I could hear the girls upstairs wowing at the house and giggling like cartoon characters.

They tumbled downstairs and helped me finish the pizza after I had told them Reg would be in overnight. They asked coyly to share the last beer after they had cracked it.

I hope he's alright," said Rhea. Little Di was stuffing pizza into her face. She was nyumming to herself, 'nyum, nyum, nyum'.

"I don't know; he didn't say," I said flatly, draining the last of my VB stubby. A silent moment, then Rhea said...

"I saw a billy you picked up outside Steve; anything to go with that?"

Yes, they had seen me take the horribly stained Orchy bottle from the driveway where Reg and I had abandoned it earlier. I thought about Reg's stash and hesitated.

"Look, it's not really mine and I know how protective he is about his stash, so maybe we'll just share a party cone." They both looked excited and I went for the pantry. They couldn't have been much older than me; eighteen or nineteen I guessed, but were obviously experienced in the ways of the world falling from one fortuitous situation to the next. Free ride, free pizza, free beer and now free cones. What a life? I was cautious and kept an eye on the bowl making sure there was going to be some left for Reg when he got home. I also knew there was whiskey in the sink cupboard but decided to see where the party cone would lead.

Well, as you know, you never imbibe after you've had too much to drink and the girls became overtly animated and insisted on going to the beach. It was a dark treacherous walk down the sandy track and the girls were making so much noise and stumbling over each other trying to hang onto my white shirt in the darkness.

Once we hit the beach they began peeling clothes off and were intent on going for a swim. I warned them it was too rough but they went in anyway. Naked, they got pounded in the shorebreak and made their way back up the beach; hair plastered with sand, giggling and began running north towards the headland.

I ran behind them watching their boobs and bums bounce up and down and to the sides until they fell exhausted on the sand, wrestled each other awkwardly and then looked back up the beach to where they had left their clothes. They stumbled back to the south, sandy and wet and beginning to shiver. As the moon was coming up over the horizon, I showed them where their clothes were and they merely picked them up and followed me back up the track to the house, naked. The whole time I was thinking that this was a dream I was having and had to keep looking back at them to make sure they were following.

Once back at the house, Di said sheepishly and shivering, "Can we have a shower?" I told them there was no hot water and together they screamed as the cold water hit them. They quickly changed back into their clothes and emerged into the kitchen where I had the kettle on. They were shivering and hugging each other for warmth in the cold concrete house. Rhea moved over to me and cuddled up from behind trying to absorb some of my heat and Di joined her. We had a brief three way cuddle but I felt like that was all it was going to be. After a cup of tea, I offered for them to sleep in Reg's room in the double bed as there were two blankets.

"What about you Steve? Where you gonna sleep?" Di asked provocatively.

I've got a room in there," I said pointing to the tiny space beside the kitchen. They both checked out my sad room and Rhea said, "You could sleep with us, to keep warm." They both smiled expecting an answer. I replied with an embarrassed face and said I would check in on them after I'd cleaned up and locked the house for the night. They trotted off to the bedroom and sank deep into Reg's bed under the doona trying to get warm. They had left a dripping, sandy mess in the bathroom and the towels were abandoned on the floor.

I cleaned my teeth, grabbed my only blanket from my room and turned out the kitchen light.

"Make room for the third little pig," I whispered as I approached the dark room.

"Over this side Steve," came Di's little voice. I slid in under the covers and instantly felt the warmth they had created. Rhea was asleep already but Di spooned me and I enjoyed feeling her body against me until she fell asleep. I lay for a long time listening to their breathing to make sure they weren't going to rob us, but of what? I had no idea. Rhea snored and Di belted her occasionally to stop the gurgling but I eventually fell asleep.

Sometime during the night my legs had tangled with Di's and her head and hand were resting on my chest. I resisted the urge to move her until the phone rang just after sunup. I leaped out of my warm and cosy crib and picked up before the third ring.

"Yeah?"

"I've got to go to Brisbane." It was Reg. "Clean up the house and go home. Leave the car at my brother's place around the corner. Take the kiff and billy with you and turn the power off. I'll be in touch; (he paused like he was medicated) and clean out the fridge."

"You alright?" I asked genuinely concerned for him and my slave job in paradise. He hung up. I had been given my orders. I made toasted stale bread with vegemite and a cup of tea. I was going through my list of things to do when I heard Rhea call out at me, "I'll have a cup Steve." "Me too," yelled Di. I was the slave again. It felt good having some company even though they were both a little strange compared to most of the girls I'd met. They seemed free and were just floating through the universe. I had no idea what they did for a living, their last names, where they actually came from but I didn't care. It was part of my ideal life in paradise. I didn't judge them for who they were (except the messy bathroom habits) and I thought about where I would go from here. I looked around the unfinished house and wondered if I would ever see it again. My short lived, ironically juxtaposed, slavery and paradise had come to an end. I offered to drive the girls to the highway but they said they would walk and thanked me with little cheek pecks as they giggled out the door.

I quickly cleaned everything on the list of 'jobs to do do before you leave paradise' and I heard the surf pounding in the distance, calling me.

It was all-time glassy and perfect 4-5 foot peeling over the bank to the south of the beach track I had run down the night before with the naked girls. I had a 5'3" Kevin Platt twin fin with no leg rope, well before Mark Richard's rode his boards to a world championship. Everyone had twin fins or single-finned 6'1" round tails or swallow tails. Even if I told any of the guys in the surf about the girls, I doubt they would have believed me so I caught every available wave for the next three hours until the southerly came up and chased us all out of the water; sometimes the ocean wants to be left alone. The quiet house welcomed me into its' unusual concrete coolness. I didn't shower but threw some more clothes on and looked in the now vacant pantry at a jar of vegemite and a packet of stale Sao's. I was so hungry I could have chewed the arse of a grilled horse through a cane chair. Don't be offended, Mr Horse ain't.

I still had some of the money Reg gave me for the pizza and calculated that I could get a bus to Brisbane and still afford a burger from the shop down the road. I was spending the last of my 'unofficial' pay that I had earnt. Was it a job? Did Reg also calculate how much it would cost for a bus ticket and a pizza or did Reg just fall off the building as an excuse to send me on my way. As I walked, I thought, 'none of the above. It's just a random moment in time, like meeting the girls last night.' I strode on towards the smell of burgers in the distance.

Sure enough, just before I reach the Sunshine Beach shops, I hear Rhea's raucous laughter accompanied by Di's complimentary cartoonic chuckles. I smile to myself thinking they are still on their 'free' roll after they left my house, 'my house?'

They are sitting with an older guy at the pie shop laughing and playing their 'free' game all over him. He's trapped but doesn't know it. He thinks he's going to have sex with one or both of them but he is sadly mistaken.

It looks like he's bought them food and drinks and I bet myself they end up at his place tonight. When they see me they wave and yell, "Hi Steve". I wave back and enter the burger store to order the Aussie Special with lettuce, tomato, cheese, egg, beetroot, bacon, steak, pineapple and extra onions; oh and barbecue sauce. It was the best three dollar burger in the world; that was closest to me. I hadn't eaten since the stale vegemite toast for breakfast and the smell of food was making my stomach growl. I waited with ticket number eight just outside the door. Li'l Di hopped over towards me smiling wide.

"What's for dinner tonight Steve?" she said, her eyebrows raised in anticipation.

"I'm going back to Brisbane tomorrow and I only have enough for a burger and a bus ticket."

She looked at me sympathetically, or maybe she had the munchies again and said cheerily,

"Ok, see ya round." She walked back to the table and whispered something to Rhea who turned and looked at me, smiling. She waved and I waved back. "Number eight," came Kev's voice from within the shop. He handed me a white paper packet with the burger inside and then winked at me and gave me a bag of hot chips as well. "Enjoy Stevie." I was stoked.

I walked home eating the hot chips and thought about what Di had said to Rhea. They know I'm leaving and that Reg is in

Brisbane. They might try to poach the house and squat til they get caught. The thought of it excited me somehow. I imagined locking up the house and them breaking in through a window somewhere and turning it into a party house. It wouldn't be my fault as long as I lock it up to the best of my ability. What could they do? Leave wet towels in the bathroom and sleep on dirty sheets? They would.

Once home and having hoovered the burger and all the juices running down my arms, I boiled the kettle, packed one and settled in for my last night in paradise. There was no TV and the collection of cassettes was all Reg's. I chose one called Tim Buckley, 'Greetings from LA' and pushed play.

The dawn came early after my dreamless sleep. I packed my clothes into an old Ansett Airlines bag, grabbed my board and locked up the house for the last time. I drove Reg's car round the block to his brother's and as I walked back past the neighbour's house I saw Chris Cornell and Stuart 'Duck' about to tip-toe down the road with their boards.

"You coming Steve?" asked Chris not stopping, "its all-time man, clean, glassy tubes.

"I've got to go to Brisbane. Reg is in hospital and he probably won't be back for a while."

Stuart, (who used to stick a hose up his arse and then spray water out of it) said, "Hope he's all good mate." He was an odd character but he and Chris were both really good surfers and knew Reg as the same. Chris went on to be one of the top ten surfers in Australia because of his radical, 'no fall off' style '. Another surfer who'd joined them, called Dominic Wybrow, had earned the nick name 'Araldite' because he also never fell off. I'm not sure why Stuart was called 'Duck'.

"Watch the house!" I yelled at them as they picked their bare feet down the sandy gravel road to the beach.

They waved back at me as I headed to the main road to hitch into town to buy a bus ticket back to Brisbane carrying my Ansett bag of possessions and my surfboard.

I know that sounds like an ending but it's really just a beginning. After 40 jobs in 40 years I realise now that I just want the same thing I had when I was 17. I had the freedom to do what I wanted, (although I was a slave of sorts) the beach, fishing and enjoying the simple pleasures in life as they unfolded. I loved the coastal banksias, casuarinas, pandanus and gums; the noisy friar birds, black cockatoos, lorikeets and Lewin honey-eaters, the ever-changing ocean and the unexpectedness of what may happen next.

All the other jobs after this were just a means to get back to that simple place where I was happiest. Not saying that other moments in my life weren't happy but I sought that solace with a passion. I read somewhere that if you follow your passion, all else will follow. They didn't say how long it would take but I think I'm getting close. All the good things are coming to me now and I couldn't be happier.

Reg eventually turned up at the unfinished house four weeks

later and found Di and Rhea firmly ensconced in the residence, having decorated it with curtains and plants and an entourage of local young miscreants. Reg and Di ended up marrying and having four children. I often ask myself, 'was that because of my random pickup that night or would they have eventually met? Was the real reason for me having that job (?) at that time to hook up Reg and Di with their eternal happiness or was that just another coincidence?'

I decided it was fate and that everyone is a victim to it; although, you can make your own fate.

• • • • •

Oh, by the way, I did become a teacher and spent thirty fulfilling years doing what I should have been doing all along. Thanks kids. Some of those students now have grandchildren.

I have embarked on another career, although I wouldn't call it a job, it's more a passion.

www.ingramcontent.com/pod-product-compliance
Lightning Source LLC
Chambersburg PA
CBHW050315010526
44107CB00055B/2245